Participatory Design and Social Transformation

Participatory Design and Social Transformation introduces theories and methodologies for using image-oriented narratives as modes of inquiry and proposition toward greater justice and equity for society and the environment.

Participatory artistic- and design-based research encounters—being, making, and learning with people, things, and situations—are explored through practices that utilize image-oriented and cinematic narratives. Collaborative alliances are invited to consider aesthetics, visuality, attunement, reflection, reciprocity, and care as a means for transdisciplinary approaches that foster generative and ethically responsible conditions toward collective liberation. The design of spectacles is proposed as a way for collective movements to affectively contribute to positive systemic changes from the ground up. In this way, *Participatory Design and Social Transformation* bridges contemporary advances in design theory and practice with media and art theory, the human and social sciences, and a pedagogy of interdependence.

Participatory Design and Social Transformation will be of great interest to both professional and academic communities, providing resources for researchers, artists, designers, activists, students, educators, and leaders engaged with initiatives for transformation.

John A. Bruce is a researcher, design strategist, educator, and filmmaker. He is Assistant Professor of Design Strategies at Parsons School of Design, USA, where he also serves as Director of the Transdisciplinary Design MFA program. He co-directed the documentary film *End of Life*, the result of four years spent with five people at various stages of dying. He was a 2015/16 Fellow at the Graduate Institute for Design Ethnography and Social Thought at The New School.

Routledge Focus on Environment and Sustainability

Mathematical Models and Environmental Change
Case Studies in Long Term Management
Douglas J. Crookes

German Radioactive Waste
Changes in Policy and Law
Robert Rybski

The Sustainable Manifesto
A Commitment to Individual, Economical, and Political Change
Kersten Reich

Phyto and Microbial Remediation of Heavy Metals and Radionuclides in the Environment
An Eco-Friendly Solution for Detoxifying Soils
Rym Salah-Tazdaït and Djaber Tazdaït

Water Governance in Bolivia
Cochabamba since the Water War
Nasya Sara Razavi

Indigenous Identity, Human Rights and the Environment in Myanmar
Local Engagement with Global Rights Discourses
Jonathan Liljeblad

Participatory Design and Social Transformation
Images and Narratives of Crisis and Change
John A. Bruce

Participatory Design and Social Transformation

Images and Narratives of Crisis and Change

John A. Bruce

Routledge
Taylor & Francis Group

LONDON AND NEW YORK

from Routledge

First published 2022
by Routledge
4 Park Square, Milton Park, Abingdon, Oxon OX14 4RN

and by Routledge
605 Third Avenue, New York, NY 10158

Routledge is an imprint of the Taylor & Francis Group, an informa business

© 2022 John A. Bruce

British Library Cataloguing-in-Publication Data
A catalogue record for this book is available from the British Library

Library of Congress Cataloging-in-Publication Data
A catalog record has been requested for this book

ISBN: 978-0-367-36525-7 (hbk)
ISBN: 978-1-032-30508-0 (pbk)
ISBN: 978-0-367-36526-4 (ebk)

DOI: 10.4324/9780367365264

Typeset in Times New Roman
by Deanta Global Publishing Services, Chennai, India

For Dennis

Contents

Figures

Prologue

In 1989/90, with an investment of a few hundred dollars, eight months of my time, and the collaborative effort of many friends, we created the film *Apple Juice*, a nine-minute participatory ethnographic film about Manhattan's skateboarding subculture. I was intrigued with the ways skaters moved across the terrain of the city in cliques comprising diverse racial and economic backgrounds, appearing and dispersing as small swarms of camaraderie, mischief, and joy. These skaters, ages ranging from young teens to early 20s, were fearless in pushing back against the barriers and enclosures of the metropolis and the trappings of approaching adulthood. I was 25 years old at the time and terrified. After five years of living what I imagined as my desired life in New York City—art school educated, emancipated and estranged from my family, and queer—the precariousness of working (if lucky) crappy jobs for little pay, residing in rat-infested apartments often without heat in the winter, facing HIV/AIDS as a potential death sentence, and an assortment of other practical and psychic navigations charged with the treacherousness of a high-wire act was debilitating. Meanwhile, the global machinations of neoliberalism and increasing corporatization, accelerated through the Regan–Bush–Thatcher agendas escalating privatization, deregulation, and austerity, cast a dark shadow over social systems for the care and well-being of people, communities, nonhumans, the planet, and cooperative ways of life. The skaters modeled a movement of defiance that served as an antidote to my shell-shocked paralysis. I hung out with them in the East Village Shop Skate NYC and in the streets, city parks, office building plazas, the base of the Brooklyn Bridge, and dozens of other spaces where the cityscape seemed "subconsciously designed as a skate park," as the film's voiceover muses (Bruce 1990). The skaters hacked and queered systems of containment, categorization, and competition through their free-form inventiveness and fluid capacities of organization. They embodied a radical symbiosis—conspiring, exchanging, reflecting, and evolving—to disregard prescriptions of market-driven conformity, reward,

Figure 0.1 John A. Bruce, (left), during the making of the film *Apple Juice*, 1989.

and punishment. And they had style. The aesthetics of their accouterments were far from team-sport uniforms with numbers and stripes.

I handed out cameras to the skaters, and they filmed each other, as shown in Figure 0.2, and sometimes me, as shown in Figure 0.1. Their curiosities concerning perspective became alive through performing from both sides of the camera—where to be and ways to see. We trusted each other, and they embraced the invitation of the process. Broken bones in my hand and ten stitches above one eye earned my street cred and snapped me out of a disso-ciated and disembodied haze. The experience of street skating in New York City in the late 1980s was a bracing lesson in what it means to be present—to show up and come together in ways free from titles, roles, or expertise; to privilege curiosity; to engage in peer-to-peer learning and co-creation; to live boldly, messily, and gracefully in a state of not knowing. Co-creating and sharing image-oriented artifacts were a means for celebrating these ways of being—reflective practices within nondiscursive exchanges. In these moments, I came to believe in the power of collective acts of making and encountering moving image narratives to spur positive change.

This small book has taken shape around the idea that images and narra-tives can provide unique value to participatory design processes engaged in efforts toward social transformation. It is an introduction to using

Figure 0.2 Skaters film each other during the making of *Apple Juice*, 1989/90.

image-oriented narratives as modes of inquiry and proposition within discursive and nondiscursive exchanges for learning through making. Collective acts of making and synthesizing images and narratives can play active roles within design processes in ways beyond serving only as a reference or record. Participatory artistic- and design-based research approaches rely on encounters—being with people, things, and situations—and embodied learning that centers attunement, reflection, reciprocity, and care. These approaches are sensorial ways of being in the world and serve collaborative efforts for sense-making and way-finding.

Throughout this book, discussions and process examples often reference the *End of Life* project—artistic research co-led by me and Paweł Wojtasik. The *End of Life* project, beginning in 2012 and ongoing, focuses on learning from experiences at the end of life as a way to glean insights to inform all stages of life and life's transitions, shown in Figure 0.3. Our participatory process relies on relationships along with the methods of video ethnography and cinematic forms of expression. Several exercises and workshop examples, as derived from experiences of the *End of Life* project, are presented as methodological approaches rather than design innovation case studies.

The discussions and process examples in this book depart from more familiar associations with notions of designing for sustainability and social innovation. This is evidenced by approaches focused on processual,

Figure 0.3 Sarah Grossman reads a book that she authored (as Miriam Cohen) to John A. Bruce, during the making of the film *End of Life*, 2017.

collaborative, and experiential possibilities for transdisciplinary praxis, bringing together ideas drawn from media theory, systems thinking, and experimental forms of social science research. The approaches are focused on expanded ways of seeing to challenge the confines of 'the problem space,' rather than 'solutions-based' didactic responses aimed at 'fixing' things. I am not focused on end results as a way to begin or maintain meaningful and participatory processes of investigation. Instead, I invest in design as an invitation for people to come together in genuine learning communities toward collective goals for greater well-being and without harm. Participatory design is an invitation for finding productivity in being uncomfortable, for working to get beyond what we think we know, together, and for acknowledging and honoring the value and fragility of interdependence. Methods and tools for research and design are shared in this book, while discussions predominantly propose conditions that affectively support capacities for new ways of seeing, being, and imagining that ultimately lead to transformations for a more equitable, just, and sustainable future. They are points of departure and welcome the participation of anyone with desires to experiment in the service of explorations for collective ways forward.

***

References

Bruce, J.A. (Director) (1990) *Apple Juice*, Train-Tracks Inc. Available at: https://vimeo.com/96353303

Bruce, J.A. and Wojtasik, P. (Directors) (2017) *End of Life*, US: Grasshopper Films.

Acknowledgments

I trek joyfully, fearlessly, and sometimes awkwardly through discussions of theory and practice in this book, having been encouraged and delighted by scholars, practitioners, students, places, animals, plants, things, and spirits. The ponderings, notions, ideas, practices, and experiences contributing to this text occurred mostly between the spring of 2013 and the fall of 2021. Writing for this book began in Syros, Greece, and ended in Oaxaca, Mexico, encouraged by soulful comrades Athina Rachel Tsangari, Ian Hassett, Katerina Bourin, Daisy Nam, a collection of cats (Aimo, Mixia, Oz, Nico, Tuxedo, and Milpa), and most of all Dennis Lim. In between those magical places, writing took place in New York City where I serve as faculty at Parsons School of Design, The New School.

My work with the *End of Life* project features prominently throughout this book and is the result of many years of collaboration with Paweł Wojtasik, a brilliant mentor who taught me what it means to truly participate, along with the collaboration of the main characters of the film *End of Life*, Matthew Freedman, Sarah Grossman (Miriam Cohen), Carol Verostek, Doris Johnson, and Ram Dass. This book would not exist without the years of collaboration I was fortunate to experience with Barbara Adams, the person most genuinely dedicated to learning I've ever known. I met Barbara when we were both awarded Fellowships with the Graduate Institute for Design Ethnography and Social Thought (GIDEST) at The New School, an experience that greatly benefitted the *End of Life* project. I am grateful to GIDEST Director Hugh Raffles for his support, along with Fellows Joseph Lemelin, Scott Brown, Radhika Subramaniam, Vicky Hattam, Michelle Weitzel, Alexios Tsigkas, Laura Y. Liu, Orit Halpren, Jilly Traganou, and others who contributed to this generative space.

I am grateful for stimulating exchanges and experiments with colleagues in and around Parsons and The New School, many of whom are also friends beyond the institution: Leo Goldsmith, Jane Pirone, Patty Beirne, Chris Fussner, Hala Malak, Lara Penin, Eduardo Staszowski, Adam Brent,

Mariana Amatullo, Anh-Ton Tran, Daye Huang, Johanna Tysk, Martin Lenon, Jenny Liu, Javi Arenas, Ankita Roy, Anze Zadel, Lisa Norton, Sam Haddix, Cynthia Lawson Jaramillo, Mark Randall, Alison Mears, Giorgio Faedo, Theo Wilkins, Jack Wilkinson, Valentina Branada Rojas, Christopher Lopez, Sophie Riendeau, Christian Smirnow, Miriam Young, V. Lee, Alexa Gantous, Nicole Anand, Mikhail Zalesky, Debbie Gibb, Eileen Vogel, Rhea Alexander, Chloe Snower, and others. A special thanks to university colleagues, and others, who fearlessly joined our weekly 'temporary autonomous zone' aka TD Coffee: Jamer Hunt, Jeongki Lim, Miriam Steele, Ben Lang, Bailey Foote, and Anna Valtonen. Thanks to spirit pals, gurus, and guides: Michele Bruce, Sandra-Lee Phipps, Daniela Alatorre, Rich Rickaby, Racheal Rakes, Nicholas Elliott, Simon Aguia, Lori Hanau, Andrea Picard, Mati Diop, Bertrand Bonello, Judith Lou Lévy, Verena Paravel, Lucien Castaing-Taylor, Joana Pimento, Stephanie Spray, Cìntia Gil, Kent Jones, Debera Johnson, Toby Lee, Kasia Plazinska, Jem Cohen, Alkis Papastathopoulos, Peter Strugatz, Steve Holmgren, Bangwei Bao, Joe Hollier, Kaiwei Tang, Jude Tallichet, Tim Spellios, Bill Morrison, Larry Greenberg, Michael Holden, Anna Ehrsam, Ellie Lee, Matthew Connelly, Jocelyn Ripley, Phil Ronniger, Francoise Jaffe, and Gus Glimis who taught me about proximity reverence.

Bowing in your directions.

1 Introduction
Images of crisis, images of change

"Photography is also an act of love." This opening line in Hervé Guibert's essay 'Ghost Image,' speaks to the generative potential of participating in the making of images (Guibert [1982] 2014). Sense-making, meaning-making, and decision-making can be readily realized through activities of encountering, creating, and sharing narratives. Stories, and especially image-oriented and sensory narrative experiences, are the heart and soul of integrative knowledge domains and the basis for thought and action. This short book explores image and narrative creations as modes of learning with the capacity to address complex social issues in the realms of art- and design-based research. For several years, I have been experimenting with cinematic tropes—the formal elements of moving images and sound that impact narrative and meaning-making—as a way of informing artistic and design-based research processes. Central to this practice-based approach are frameworks I refer to as *images of crisis* and *images of change*—ways of seeing, understanding, and acting that address what, in design syntax, are commonly referred to, respectively, as 'the problem space' and 'ways forward.' These methods are particularly salient within transdisciplinary investigations and propositions focused on transformations of greater environmental and social justice.

The approaches shared in this book introduce and prioritize modes of a sensory exchange over didactic language-based forms of communication. Embodied learning relies on what appears to us through our senses, minds, and hearts. Appearances are the ways in which images become evident and serve the activities of meaning-making. What is apparent is not always true, and what is true is not always apparent. Images—whether sensorily, relived as memories, or encountered as mediated artifacts through art, design, cinema, television, print media, the Internet, and other visual forms—are never capable of exacting complete or fixed truths. All the while, images that circulate widely or with strong resonance among individuals and the publics can serve as powerful levers for shifting cultural understandings

DOI: 10.4324/9780367365264-1

and opinions. It is this malleable nature of our relationship with images that presents a great opportunity for working with visual artifacts and narratives within participatory research and design processes. The discussions in this book use the term 'design process' to refer to approaches for addressing complex social issues. These processes center artistic and design-based transdisciplinary research and practices—the "systemic use of methods that make the most of creative imagination" while leveraging the depth across and beyond disciplinary knowledge—a kind of 'exploratory social sciences' (and humanities, I might add), as described by Geoff Mulgan in his discussion paper "The Case for Exploratory Social Sciences," published by The New Institute (Mulgan 2021, p. 6). The 'creativity methods' outlined by Mulgan are similar to those familiar to transdisciplinary design researchers: deep play with abstract models, provocative prototypes (provotypes), grafting ideas or analogues from one field to another, experimental journey mapping, design futures and speculative fiction, and so on (Mulgan 2021). These methodologies might be exploited in significant ways through narratology and especially through visual applications.

Jargon and other highly specialized forms of language can create barriers to the ways we might learn within research and design processes by limiting the inclusion, agency, and efficacy of collaboration. This book introduces ideas and methods for working with visual and image-oriented narratives through making, sharing, and manipulating images and narratives to investigate, imagine, and manifest more equitable and sustainable futures. Specifically, it asks: How might practitioners of participatory research and design experiment with expanded notions of appearance, disappearance, and reappearance for embodied learning and new ways of knowing?

In Hervé Guibert's essay 'Ghost Image,' a teenage son, Guibert, carefully stages the photographic portrait of his mother (Guibert [1982] 2014). The living room furniture is rearranged to create a more spacious atmosphere, a particular angle is chosen where the light is more flattering, and the mother's clothing and hair style are adjusted to reflect an earlier, free-spirited period of her life. The father is barred from the photo session by the son so that his mother performs outside of her role as 'wife.' In the story, the young photographer works to design conditions for the emergence of the woman who otherwise could not appear within the family home. He bears witness to this appearance, made visible through the photographic moment. His efforts to conjure the appearance of the past expose the dimensions of his desire for knowledge that might inform a new way forward in their relationship. When it is later discovered that the film had not been properly loaded into the camera and that no images had been recorded from the session, curiosity is heightened. Ghosts, or ghost images, are an invitation to potential learning. Haunting is the appearance of traces that persist in the absence of fully recognizable images while illuminating histories of the present that provoke inquiry and considerations for future trajectories. Capacities for reading ghostly traces, free from assumed, concretized, and foreclosed meanings, inspire an embrace of groundlessness necessary for imaginative and fearless learning—ways for moving beyond what we think we already know.

Getting beyond what we think we know, together

Collaborative thought and action that provide conditions for atmospheres of emergence have the potential to spur collective effervescence and ideally move us toward collective liberation. It is important to consider the notion of emergence as that which might bubble up—uniquely come to be—as a result of certain atmospheres and might appear in ways that are beyond recognizable understandings of the current conditions. Challenges to remaining open to what might emerge are often brought about by propensities to focus on familiar things and patterns, entrenched notions of causal relationships, and preconceived expectations or anticipated outcomes, all of which can foreclose ways of seeing new possibilities. Herein lies a critical tension for design researchers between what we think we know and what we might seek to transgress. Narratology offers perspectives that can inform methodologies for participatory research and design, particularly through working with tropes that illuminate the unfolding of events and aspects of their causal histories along with intimations constellating desires. Compelling narratives might be shaped by that which is apparent and also by that which is *hinted at*—perhaps the emergence of haunting or fragmentary anticipation—and experienced through sensing, *feeling*, possibilities. Certain forms of narrative affect can be utilized as ways to motivate aspirations for transformation, similar to notions of queerness as described by José Esteban Muñoz,

> that thing that lets us feel that this world is not enough, that indeed something is missing. Often we can glimpse the worlds proposed and promised by queerness in the realm of the aesthetic. The aesthetic, especially the queer aesthetic, frequently contains blueprints and schemata of a forward-dawning futurity.
>
> (Muñoz 2019, p. 1)

The film *Lovers Rock*, by the artist and filmmaker Steve McQueen, is a wonderful visceral example of *emergence* and, in particular, of an emergent moment of collective effervescence for collective liberation. Set in 1980 west London, the film takes place over the course of a weekend. The centerpiece event is a Saturday night house party where members of the city's West Indian community gather to eat, drink, and dance, having been barred from white nightclubs. *Lovers Rock* is named after a genre of music—a romantic, hyperfeminine subcategory of reggae, popularized by Black Londoners in the mid-1970s (Harris 2020; McQueen 2020). The dance party generates a lush atmosphere of dimly lit colors, textures, and movements that climaxes during the song "Silly Games," an anthem of the *Lovers Rock* genre. When the song ends, the gyrating dancers continue signing a cappella, their feet on the dancefloor creating the only other sounds. The scene is more than a representation—it is an authentically co-created moment that illuminates collective effervescence—embodied transcendence, camaraderie, and joy—that stretches toward a forward-dawning futurity, beyond oppressive systems, and beyond movie-making expectations, "I'm not too sure what it was, but there was a spiritual element to it," McQueen says. "I can't put my finger on it. It was beautiful" (Harris 2020). McQueen describes his job with *Lovers Rock*,

> Directing the actors simply meant creating an environment where he was an observer of every blushing face, every small drama, the sweating walls, the singing chorus. "To see Black women looking at other Black women and feeling acknowledgment."
>
> (Harris 2020)

The embodied learning that takes place in the making of *Lovers Rock* and especially the climactic scene described by McQueen as 'spiritual' are models for ways design processes, as reflective practices embracing non-preconception, might allow for emergence—to cede the dominance of consciousness to the movements and senses of the body and, perhaps, beyond the body—to feel through incorporeal states of being.

Working with narrative—whether co-creating stories or collective encounters with stories—is central to the theories and practices of participatory research and design and is particularly salient for ethical considerations regarding efforts toward greater social and environmental justice. Investigations in the service of addressing complex social issues demand more than steps in identifying problems in order to propose solutions—what is often typical of research *for* design. Participation is not limited to fieldwork. The analysis and synthesis of findings from participatory research rely upon messy and meandering work—reflective, iterative, and bespoke approaches—and is perhaps best categorized not in terms of tools or methods but as multimodal ways of being with narrative. A complex situation comprises multiple perspectives, divergent stakes, and competing goals and, like a narrative account, evolves through a number of ongoing causal relationships, potentially across various spaces and nonlinear time. Image-oriented and narrative experiments for building capacities to design the design process co-creatively are further examined in Chapter 2 of this book, 'Proximity and Duration, Senses and Images.'

Narrative is not an informational set of instructions like a weather report or a recipe. Stories—whether in the form of images, sounds, or written and spoken language—can be spectacles of open-ended provocation and might present elements that are true and false, and fact and fiction, and refer to time and space across a spectrum of the past, present, and future. The unfolding of causal relationships is central to what constitutes narrative, and these revelations can be dramatic, humorous, shocking, thrilling, meditative, and so on. Narrative can direct and misdirect our attention, as in a magician's sleight of hand or a joke with a strategy. Learning relies on the ways we might pay attention to our attention; as learners we must iteratively reflect and not only consume. Engaging with stories, we are never completely outside of them or inside of them; we reverberate as a relational part of the *storyworld* no matter how distant, strange, or novel. At the same time, there is often a propensity to complete and make firm a singular set of meanings as gleaned from our participation with narratives, and this rush to erase mystery, perhaps to ameliorate anxiousness and fear, forecloses more expansive possibilities. The four chapters of this book propose ways that images and narratives might serve as thresholds for participatory research—to expand collective memory, understanding, and imagination—and not simply serve as references.

Efforts of artistic and design-based research dedicated to contributing to a more equitable and sustainable future demand asking the important and complicated questions of 'why, what, and with whom' before getting caught up in the questions of 'how.' Ethicist Dr Bill Grace told a story during a visit to the Bainbridge Graduate Institute on Bainbridge Island, Washington, in the autumn of 2007 that I witnessed and paraphrase here:

> Aliens from outer space land on Earth and announce that they've been observing us for a long time, and that based on what they've learned about our current systems – the appalling ways humans have treated the planet, nonhuman life, and each other, they will obliterate the planet – vaporize the whole thing to space dust. The leaders of Earth snap out of their usual infighting to band together and beg the aliens for mercy: "Wait! Give us a chance." The aliens say, "OK, here's a deal: we'll give you one year to straighten out the mess you've made. We'll be back, and if you haven't fixed it by then we'll erase you from the universe." The Earth leaders are relieved for a moment, and then panic sets in: "Wait! Tell us how we will know that we've fixed things in the right

way." The aliens look at one another with eye-rolling smirks: "When we return a year from now you need to be OK with us picking up any one of your children and moving them to any place on the planet."

(Grace 2007)

The story shared by Dr Bill Grace invites attention through familiar and unfamiliar images and provokes imagination by fracturing the certainty of what we think we know—opens up cracks for new light to shine through, illuminating the otherwise shadowy areas where accountability might be obscured. Ethics might be understood as the recognition that we, as humans, will do harm, and given this we are accountable and responsible to make the greatest efforts possible to repair the damages resulting from harm and to prevent it from occurring again. These recognitions and efforts, like narrative, are not effective in forms that resemble weather reports or recipes. I propose that design for social change can learn a great deal from narratology and find effectiveness through the use of narrative in active, collaborative, and experimental ways. The discussions and examples in this book emphasize the affective role of co-creating images and narratives through discursive and nondiscursive exchanges in ways that operate most powerfully not as equations but rather in forms more akin to a Buddhist koan.

The impacts of context on the meaning and transformative power of images and narratives are a critical consideration for design processes. The scene as described below is presented intentionally without any framing. Pedagogically, I prefer that audiences experience this narrative in its original form as a video of moving images and sounds. However, addressing readers of this book I must offer written text as an encounter.

The image of an old, white, man with a small round bandage on his nose fills the frame in medium close-up – head and shoulders. His eyes are blue, and his beard is grey. Dark age spots are visible on his bald head, revealed each time he moves to gaze downward. He wears a pale blue shirt. The background is a soft-focused off-white wall and includes one edge of what might be a gold-framed picture. He stares directly back at the viewer and only occasionally and briefly averts his eyes. The man's breathing is audible along with distant sounds of birdsong and the motion of water. At one moment, the sound of nearby wind chimes gently erupts. He strokes his beard and takes a sip, once from a glass of water that he brings into the frame from off-screen after clearing his throat. For more than six minutes the only action of the scene are these simple gestures, except for several moments when he seems to be about to speak. Each time that he nearly utters a word, he stops before saying anything. During one of these aborted speech moments, it seems that he chooses not to speak because of the sound of an airplane passing overhead – his eyes turn upward in the direction of the airplane sound and then back to the viewer, accompanied by what seems to be a conspiratorial smile. Otherwise, motivations for his pauses to speak remain mysterious. Finally, when he does speak, he says, "in our culture almost everyone is afraid of death" (Bruce, Wojtasik 2017).

The scene, as a video clip, is presented as part of an exercise I have designed for building capacities of reflection through embodied learning supported by sensorial cinematic engagements. No information about the video is provided to participants before the scene is shown. The only instruction given at the start of the exercise is to pay close attention to the six-and-a-half-minute duration of the recording.

In what ways are we conscious and unconscious of consuming and processing images and narratives that we encounter? How might we confront—*pay attention to*—ourselves and our roles as collaborators of meaning-making in and through narratives?

I have employed this exercise with diverse audiences on dozens of occasions, beginning in 2014 when the video was created by me and my collaborator Paweł Wojtasik as part of our research and film projects exploring experiences at the end of life. The exercise provides opportunities for nondiscursive sensory encounters. Participants including students, scholars, and practitioners from a wide variety of disciplines and industries have experienced a range of reactions, from perplexed and annoyed to profoundly intrigued. Frequently, responses have included speculations that the man's cognitive abilities might be impaired or that he had been asked not to speak by the makers of the video. Some viewers were made to feel uncomfortable by the experience, citing the man's struggle as a provocation of their own feelings of anxiety and fragility, while others shared that the six-and-a-half-minute encounter provided a sense of tranquility. Many viewers reported that their senses had been dramatically elevated, having become hyper-aware of sounds and movements in the room and of their own bodies. Others experienced an increased sense of wonder about certain detailed moments within the video—the pronounced sound of the man's swallowing, the uneven shape of his smile, the iridescent blue of his eyes—and related how this expanded their considerations around possible meanings of the scene. The sense of anticipation is palpable for most who engage with the video, not only in terms of the bodily gestures signaling, in prolonged and arrested attempts, that the man is about to speak, but also the rush to make sense of the scene—to anticipate what might emerge by way of codifying the available information. Much of human existence is motivated by thought and action in the service of anticipation, and capacities for these activities rely on the ways we might expand ways of seeing, feeling, and analyzing information. Joan Didion eloquently states,

> We interpret what we see, select the most workable of the multiple choices. We live entirely, especially if we are writers, by the imposition of a narrative line upon disparate images, by the "ideas" with which we have learned to freeze the shifting phantasmagoria which is our actual experience.
>
> (Didion 1979, p. 11)

Experiences with the video provoke a variety of sensory attunements and create channels—invitations—to enter the unique atmosphere represented in the video and to confront both the mystery of the other and the self, challenging assumptions and allowing for the discovery of new perspectives with greater imagination.

Spoiler alert. The man in the video is Ram Dass, as shown in Figure 1.1, who had been a well-known spiritual teacher in the United States and had brought Eastern thought to the Western world through his talks, practices, and books. Ram Dass dedicated much of his life and work to explorations of higher consciousness and what it means to be truly present—to *just be*, as well as how we might foster healthier relationships within consciousness

Figure 1.1 Ram Dass from the film *End of Life* by John Bruce and Paweł Wojtasik, 2017.

of our mortality. His book *Be Here Now*, a best-seller when published in 1971, continues to be widely read. The six-and-a-half-minute video is an excerpt from the feature-length film *End of Life*, co-directed by me, with Paweł Wojtasik, and is part of artistic research that includes short films, performances, installations, and collaborations with studio courses at Parsons School of Design (Bruce, Wojtasik 2017).

Our relationship with Ram Dass evolved rather quickly, and we were able to establish a degree of trust that enabled us to invite him to engage in co-creative experiments of nondiscursive exchange. Our process of video ethnography was minimal—all technical operations were managed by us, with no additional people, supporting an intimate atmosphere of exchange. The audio and video gear we used was compact and unobtrusive to reduce distractions and barriers. Initially, our process assumed a typical semi-structured interview format, engaging Ram Dass in discussions on his perspectives on mortality and his experiences of being with people in the process of dying. Ram Dass had given perhaps hundreds of talks and interviews during the several decades of his life as a public figure. These well-documented expressions reveal his great talent to discursively share insightful and passionate perspectives on existence. Listening to Ram Dass speak had become a cult phenomenon among certain communities of spirituality seekers. However, as participatory researchers, our curiosity was centered on how we might co-create conditions for nondiscursive exchanges addressing our presence with mortality.

Our first nondiscursive experiment with Ram Dass invited everyone in the room to meditate for 12 minutes, while our cameras were operating unattended. The experience opened a way of being together without the need for spoken language. Our attunement relied on paying attention to our own and each other's bodies as forms of expression that invited exchange. Following this experiment, we asked Ram Dass to guide us on a journey from a place of fear and anxiety around dying to a place of grace and invited him to use words or not use words. The six-and-a-half-minute video described above is the beginning segment of a 35-minute recording of this experiment. During the process of creating the video, Ram Dass addressed me with his gaze while I kneeled facing him, next to one of our cameras. My experience during the 35 minutes of recording, having arrived at this particular moment after many hours over the course of two days with Ram Dass, is not represented or explained by the video that was produced. The video is a co-created artifact from the experience and possesses its own affect. Our work as design researchers centered on creating the conditions for a particular atmosphere that was conducive for emergence. Participatory practices privilege and place trust in co-creative, open-ended, presence, rather than preconceived ideas, agendas, or anticipation of outcomes. Being present does not mean 'it's all about me.' Ram Dass reminds us that "The ego is one of the selves." "This one," he says, his hand touching his forehead, as shown in Figure 1.1, "and this one," his hand moving to the middle of his chest (Bruce, Wojtasik 2017). The spirit, Ram Dass teaches, moves between the head and the heart, as well as beyond the body. "I am not Ram Dass," he tells me, "Ram Dass is a figure walking, up ahead. I am loving awareness."

How might we, as design researchers, participate with people and situations in ways that avoid, or at least reduce, unproductive distancing, reductive didacticism, and the limits of language? How might overcoming these relied upon approaches open new modes that foster emergence, co-creative experiments, and embodied learning? How might we more intentionally engage our senses to allow relationships to form and unfold from a place that privileges our presence as humans rather than our roles, titles, or expertise? Franco Bifo Berardi, in referencing the Wittgenstein quote "the limits of my language are the limits of my world," suggests that the capacity to elaborate ideas toward a more equitable and sustainable future—a place beyond the seeming confines of contemporary conditions—requires language that is not limited to information or contemporary logics (Wittgenstein 1921; Berardi 2012). Berardi proposes experiments with poetical expressions that provoke the emergence of new forms toward a shared and preferable future that is "inscribed in the present reality, inscribed in the daily existence of society ... inscribed in the intellectual activity of millions of artists and cognitive workers in the world, but is hidden, impeached, suppressed, compressed by the limits of our language" (Berardi 2017). Berardi proposes that perhaps one of the most critical programs for transformation is the creation of spaces where poets and engineers can meet and exchange (Berardi 2017). How might we work to make the potential value that is inscribed in the present situation through poetic images, or the illegible resonance, more legible as an indication of paths toward a preferable future?

Design as invitation

Design, when carried out through expressions of *invitation*—the initiation of relationships within reciprocal curiosity and care—is no longer an outside agent of change and instead operates through the holistic participation with people and things, negating the divide of subject and object. Participation, as a design process with goals of transformation for a more just and equitable society, is contingent on how we *show up* to be with one another, to be with situations and things—with open minds, hearts, and senses—and how we might allow for emergence within these relationships. Participating in these ways is collaborative and co-creative rather than extractive. Together, participants engage in embodied learning for new ways of knowing. In this way, transformations are guided by shared vision, shared leadership, and shared commitments to caring, compassion, and building belonging toward collective liberation. Genuine participation in the day-to-day lives of people and things will inevitably demand moving across different domains of knowledge—different disciplinary spaces with an array of past, present, and potential future interconnectedness. The capacities for supporting participation are not 'soft skills' as traditional disciplines have often defined them and are rather the uniquely core strengths of transdisciplinary ways of being within efforts of transformation.

Transdisciplinarity has been discussed as an approach for problem-focused collaborative research addressing wicked problems since the early 1970s, with the origins of the phrase 'transdisciplinary' credited to Swiss philosopher and psychologist Jean Piaget who used it to describe research interactions without disciplinary boundaries (Klein 2018; Piaget 1972, cited in Nicolescu 2007). Now, in the third decade of the 21st century, it is even more widely understood that change toward greater equity and justice for social, environmental, and economic conditions requires working across and beyond disciplinary boundaries. The challenges at hand are global, complex, and dynamic.

Central to transdisciplinary research are efforts to understand values within situated contexts and how these are informed by fundamental human factors—aesthetics, ethics, and conceptual attitudes of people and societal groups. Yet these factors are too often eclipsed by attentions that are focused on the technical and practical expressions surrounding social and environmental challenges (Lawrence 2018). Designing ways forward that are inclusive and equitable requires engagements and exchanges among multicultural knowledge domains—'a trans-anthropo-logic'—the term Roderick J. Lawrence uses to describe holistic efforts toward a more sustainable future (Lawrence 2018).

The prefix 'trans' is borrowed from the Latin *trāns*, commonly understood to mean 'across,' 'through,' or 'beyond' (trans 2010). Transdisciplinary investigations and interventions *beyond* disciplines are perhaps more salient as efforts for transformation than simply moving across disciplines (Ison 2018). How might participatory praxis operate within spaces which have not been previously mapped or made accessible through established disciplines, ideologies, or institutions? In what ways might the ethical parameters and considerations be understood and navigated responsibly in spaces beyond precedents for conduct and care? How might these movements into the *beyond* (and also, as noted above, that which is already present but suppressed) present risks—challenges including dismissive or unfavorable judgments and punishments from established disciplinary positions? Halberstam's critique of disciplines is refreshingly terse,

> We may, ultimately, want more undisciplined knowledge, more questions and fewer answers. Disciplines qualify and disqualify, legitimate and delegitimate, reward and punish; most important, they statically reproduce themselves and inhibit dissent.
>
> (Halberstam 2011, p. 10)

Transdisciplinary research processes are often not easy, pleasant, or clear and are not dissimilar, at times, to the activities of explorers or investigative journalists. Participating in transdisciplinary endeavors might assume a variety of forms along a spectrum of experience types, from practical, technical, and procedural to mysterious, meta-physical, and spiritual. In my role as the Director of the Transdisciplinary Design MFA program at Parsons School of Design, I often encounter new students who arrive with romantic notions of transdisciplinary design as creative acts of 'helping' or saving people, creatures, and things from the suffering caused by our most intractable problems. While well intentioned, these dispositions can get in the way of building capacities most often demanded by the practice—patience, rigor, audacity, humility, etc., as well as tenacity for finding productivity in being uncomfortable, confused, and even disillusioned at times.

The capacity to share perspectives and ideas, including and beyond language, is at the heart of conditions for transgressing disciplinary and cultural boundaries. Image-oriented narratives can serve as invitations for imagining new expressions of value and futures for surviving and thriving beyond systems of oppression. Transdisciplinary research and design rely on challenging assumptions around ways of seeing, ways of hearing, and ways of expressing and exchanging ideas and information. These are acts of translation and co-creation that begin with gestures of invitation, and proceed at the speed of trust.

Krisis and the value of the illegible

In Greek, crisis (krísis, κρίσῐς) is a state of being that demands a decision or determination. From the root κρίνω (krīnō, "I decide") plus -σῐς (-sis), *krisis* is also linked to a moment of extreme opportunity. The word 'crisis' in late Middle English referred to a turning point of a disease. Later, as the meaning evolved beyond illness, the crisis became most understood as the point at which change must occur, for better or worse. A moment of crisis is a convergence of elements in dynamic relationships—a point within a complex system at the intersection of multiple causal forces and possibilities—where perspectives of the past, present, and future coexist with the potential to fuel narratives informing thought and action for change.

Visual narrative devices can help to illuminate moments of crisis, or *krisis*, in ways that provide design researchers with thickly detailed perspectives of complex social issues and ideally open channels for appropriate modes of engagement. Specifically, the narrative elements of a cinematic scene—moving images and sounds representing people or person-like characters engaged in relationships within a particular setting and situation—can most vividly reveal a moment of crisis. Historical events and emergent stakes might contribute to an array of motivating logics, feelings, and strategies that unfold during a cinematic scene. There are substantive differences between a scene and a story. A story might contain many scenes, and contained within each scene parts of the story are present. Similarly, a philosophical perspective of systems theory refers to something that is simultaneously a part and a whole as a *holon*, as coined by Arthur Koestler from the Greek *holos*, meaning whole and combined with the suffix *on*, indicating a particle or part (Koestler 1967). In his book *The Ghost in the Machine*, Koestler argues that there are no absolute 'parts' or 'wholes' and proposes that elements of a system are best understood as relative 'sub-wholes' within hierarchies. He describes this as the two faces of the Roman God Janus: one face looking inward at the subordinate parts that make one body a self-contained whole and the other face looking outward to society and the environment, casting the body as a part of larger systems (Koestler 1967). This notion is also described by C. Wright Mills as the task and promise of the sociological imagination, a way of being that is contingent on the capacity to "grasp history and biography and the relations between the two within society" (Mills [1959] 2000, p. 6). Our tendencies to see and judge things as either wholes or parts are entrenched and are perhaps motivated by a desire to expedite and control change by separating elements from complex systems as one might manipulate ingredients in a recipe. This kind of segregation creates silos—fragmented views of the sub-whole parts of a system—and obscures relational dynamics that are integral to the unique essence of each part. In this way, possibilities for gleaning genuine insight are diminished by limited perspectives that privilege isolation as a strategy for identifying and controlling uncertainty. Visually, this kind of segregation might be imagined as a photographic portrait rendered with a long focal length lens—a view with a tight perspective and shallow depth of field, rendering a singular object as legible through selective focus and separated from the larger field of objects, as these remain out of focus or blurry. Alternatively, a wide-angle lens allows for a more inclusive field of vision with all objects in focus, thus rendering an image that makes it more difficult to discern parts from the whole. The potential confusion brought about by complex systems can easily provoke an eagerness for clarity through isolation. Efforts for controlling chaos might, understandably, spur initial actions toward greater legibility—casting a bright light in the darkness, illuminating the edges of scale and scope, and sharpening the definitions and dimensions of things to inform how best to address them. It is no wonder that strategic approaches might aspire to acts of isolation for identifying *the* problem and designing *the* solution. At the same time, the liabilities of reductionist perspectives are evident.

Let's consider other manifestations of ways of seeing that produce and engage with both legibility and illegibility. Jack Halberstam, in his book *The Queer Art of Failure*, discusses the notion of 'legibility' as proposed by James C. Scott in terms of the dangers that arise when ways of seeing are informed by bold narratives constructed from limited perspectives, ignoring other sources of local and situated knowledge (Scott 1999, as cited in Halberstam 2009). Scott's book, *Seeing Like a State: How Certain Schemes to Improve the Human Condition Have Failed*, defines a certain kind of legibility as the imposition of differentiated order through hierarchical manipulations that resist the fuzzy and unruly realities of complex social systems (Scott 1999, as cited in Halberstam 2011). In this way, legibility might be understood as the stories told by authoritarian sources that function as dominant narratives and serve to awaken and seduce constituents yearning for logics that reflect their own opinions, defend their positions of privilege, and affirm (and perhaps fuel) their fears and insecurities. Legibility that is broad and bold in these ways obscures other narratives that might be present and vital. Traditionally, these hyper-legible conditions had been commonly understood as dominant news cycles or media noise, while the affective force of Twitter swarms, Facebook echo chambers, runaway Substacks, and the like have dramatically complicated the game of legibility.

Is seeing believing? Narratives created and circulated in response to the Covid-19 pandemic are rich with examples of the ways legibility and illegibility can be manipulated to decouple the senses from sense-making. A story appearing in the *Washington Post* in November 2020 reported that hospitals in South Dakota reached capacity for treating Covid patients, while the South Dakota Governor opposed mandates for wearing protective masks and other preventative measures despite increasing infections in the state (Villegas 2020). Nearly a year after the *Washington Post* report, an article appeared in the *Guardian* on September 29, 2021, reporting that while rates of infection were declining in the United States, with California having the lowest rate in the country at that time, counties in California's vaccine-resistant Central Valley and rural north continued to be overwhelmed with Covid illnesses and deaths; a local doctor shared that he "regularly sees patients who are on ventilators and still do not believe they have Covid-19"

(Singh 2021). These accounts reveal, in startling ways, oppositional forces to the potentiality of embodied learning. Believing demands capacities to see in more fulsome ways—through experiences free from the blinding bright light of certain narratives made hyper-legible as a mechanism of power. Motivations to act are informed through sense-making attempts—narratives—driven by needs, desires, and fears in response to a plethora of conditions of a complex world and compounded by the complexity of narrative possibilities.

How might we use narratives in ways that fortify capacities to understand, confront, and impact transformations that value collective liberation?

Ghost images and ideal types

Ghosts are in the business of haunting. Scary movies too quickly connect the actions of ghosts with nefarious agendas, while haunting might instead be understood within the context of extreme opportunity as defined by *krisis*. Ghosts, according to Avery Gordon, possess qualities to lead us toward places of transformation and healing by supporting ways to imagine what was desired and lost even though such things had never existed (Gordon 2008). Ghosts are not people who have disappeared and are rather representatives of that which is longing to appear—to be made visible and manifest in a world in need of conditions to support change. Ghost Images and Ideal Types is the name I devised for an image-oriented exercise that was originally called the Wheel of Reasoning (WOR)—a tool for identifying relationships of a problem space in order to examine possible paths toward change, developed by Freedom Lab (Freedom Lab 2007).

The WOR comprises eight wedges of a pie diagram: the first half, numbered one through four, are Cause, Threat, Problem, and Crisis; and the second half, wedges five through eight, are Source, Opportunity, Solution, and Change. The original instructions for using the WOR direct the process to begin with the section of the diagram labeled 'crisis'—the fourth wedge of the pie diagram. Considering the area of inquiry and data gathered to date for a given research endeavor, the first step is to describe the symptoms of a problem, and then work backward from 'crisis' (wedge #4 of the diagram) to 'problem' (wedge #3 of the diagram)—naming the leverage point that is producing the symptom of the crisis, followed by 'threat' (wedge #2 of the diagram) the conditions that fueled the emergence of the problem, and the considering a higher level origin—the 'cause' (wedge #1 of the diagram), that served as the fertile ground for threats to develop. A helpful way to think about the meaning of the different nodes of the tool is to look consider them in relational pairs in regard to how they are organized directly across from one another: cause/source, threat/opportunity, problem/ solution, crisis/change.

I have modified the original instructions of the WOR to encourage the use of cinematic visualizations within the wedges, or nodes, of 'crisis' and 'change,' what I refer to as 'images of crisis' and 'images of change.' Prompts for describing an 'image of crisis,' or *krisis*, and an 'image of change' invite these moments to be articulated as though one were thickly describing a five-minute scene from a film. Who are the characters within the situation? What relationship dynamics are active among them? What are the particular details of their setting? What particular actions and energetic atmospheres are alive at this moment? In what ways is time experienced and unfolding? What goals and agendas are known or unknown, and by whom? What is immanent?

The elements that we gather through our senses—what we find out through experiences—are translated into images and narratives serving as remembrances for our referential use in the future. The aesthetics of cinema utilize configurations of sights and sounds as proxies for lived experiences that trigger sense-making within our referential capacities. Cinematic narratives rely on the affective aesthetics of color, light, motion, composition, focus, sound, setting, costume, etc.—mise-en-scéne, meaning everything in the scene—in addition to people and their words and actions. A particular scene might feature a certain quality of light and a certain palette of colors in the setting, set dressing, or wardrobe. The composition of a frame—the organization and confines of what can be seen—might be busy with many things in a wide-angle focus; alternatively, it might isolate an object within a tighter frame and narrower focus. The textures of a scene are further revealed through sounds both diegetic and nondiegetic, from sources seen or unseen: the voices of people, the rumble of a passing train, birdsong, music that plays in a room or features omnipotently. These elements are nodes, or sub-wholes, of a complex system, having their own semiotic relevance and also contributing to the creation of new meanings through their participation within the scene.

Let's consider a hypothetical example. When examining the complex ecosystem of a particular community experiencing a high incidence of cancer, the 'image of crisis' might be a scene in a hospital room: a person whose body is in decline, the apparatus of medical rescue surrounding them; perhaps doctors and nurses tend to the body in decline with loved ones nearby, clearly sensing the trauma of the situation. The scene is potentially much more than a patient, a doctor, and family members and is thickly alive through our senses: the sounds of respirator machines, the smells of disinfectant, the powder-blue and putty-colored surfaces, the clinical white light illuminating rust-colored stains on the surgeon's sea-foam scrubs, the view from the hospital room window, the cadence of medical terminology delivered by experts mingled with announcements over the public address system, and so on. The image of crisis becomes inclusive of these details rendered as a scene from a movie—the mise-en-scéne expands the critical points of information and allows for greater recognition of situated knowledges. The body in decline is the center of this particular 'image of crisis.' What has brought us to this moment are the causal elements of a complex system. The notion of what is 'the problem' is perhaps not clearly evident in the 'image of crisis' within the scene as described for the sake of this example. Perhaps the doctors know that the body in decline suffers from cancer. Perhaps lung cancer. We might cite cancer as 'the problem' while that begs the question of 'how did we get to cancer?' Problems arise from conditions that threaten certain situations, in this case threaten health. In this example, the community that exhibits a high rate of illness is the place to look for what might be contributing to these conditions operating as threats. For the sake of this example, instead of just citing smoking as the threat, let's instead look at something more complex such as the incidence of resided in housing located next to a polluting factory. The factory that pollutes in close proximity to where people live is the source of the conditions that threaten health. We might 'zoom out' even further and ask, what are the conditions that brought about this particular threat? Why does a factory exist that pollutes and compromises the health of people living in close proximity? The higher level of causality, in this particular example, might be a lack of regulation and a failure of urban planning and initiatives for public health. Engaging, as a starting point, with an 'image of crisis' of real or realistic people in a detailed situation as it unfolds in real time, we can begin to see through a more careful and inclusive root–cause analysis of the relationships among day-to-day details of how people live and the greater systems that impact their lives.

Salient questions of inquiry reside in systemic factors which are often less visible. Ghosts carry forth factors of a wider historical problem space from the past as these persist in the present, albeit perhaps within confusing or ethereal states of appearance. The classic scary movie idea of a ghost might be the person who was murdered at home, and their restless soul continues to bang around the house. The haunting activities are not the problem and are rather the invitation to investigate in efforts to solve the mystery of the murder and perhaps prevent future, similar acts of violence. In the example of our patient, if we were to simply focus on a cure for cancer, we would not necessarily be addressing the systemic conditions that brought about this moment of crisis. While we desire a cure for cancer, the design research project at hand is to address the conditions which continue to bring about the emergence of the disease.

Ghosts are the reappearance of unfinished business and situated knowledges—the poetic and layered palimpsest of time and space providing ways to see the details of historical, systemic, and complex social issues—that may have become obscured by contemporary appearances of hyper-legibility. A five-minute cinematic scene is both legible and illegible. A ghost image, attempting to make itself known and struggling to appear, illuminates the 'image of crisis' and provides signifiers that allow others to relate to the situation while also alluding to questions, things hinted at and out of reach, to be pursued through further research. The first half of Ghost Images and Ideal Types is akin to the investigative work of the social sciences—attempts to understand a present situation or state of being by examining past–present moments as a way for reading the traces of conditions that have brought about an 'image of crisis.' Similarly, design research approaches investigate conditions to explore the root causes, while also seeking, even if imperfectly, to propose ways forward (Hunt 2010).

The second half of the exercise Ghost Images and Ideal Types engages a process for looking forward from the 'image of crisis' and toward a desirable future—the 'image of change.' Borrowing from theories and practices of speculative design, backcasting, and other methods for futures forecasting, the process for designing an 'image of change' invites an imagined and fulsome construction of a desired situation, replete with the same kinds of cinematic details as outlined for creating an 'image of crisis.' From my many years of experience in using Ghost Images and Ideal Types, participants seem to have greater abilities for envisioning crisis than they do for imagining a preferable future. The narratives of wicked problems can remain dominant, and thus notions of change are often only seen as problems to be solved.

An ideal type, as described originally by Max Weber, is an abstraction created in order to envision figures or states of being in comparison to aspects of the real world (Weber 1959, cited in Bruun 2016). According to Weber, an ideal type is an analytical construct—an assembled selection of traits found in reality, serving as a way to measure historical configurations, and also "as a help to sharpening 'the judgment [of scholars] concerning causal imputation'" (Weber 1959, p. 90, cited in Bruun 2016, p. 218). The idea of 'causal imputation' as a function of ideal types points to the capacity for ascribing particular value to the construct by inference from the value of the elements to which it contributes. The first half of Ghost Images and Ideal Types—activities for mapping the richness of an ecosystem and root–cause analysis within a variety of proximal and historical machinations—serves to inform, albeit without precise calculation, the formation of a mental model illuminated through an 'image of change.' One of the primary objectives of the exercise Ghost Images and Ideal Types is to surface causal relationships through working with narrative elements. However, the linkages revealed with the greatest potential for insight are often fuzzy, messy, and less didactic than what might be expected from a process for logical reasoning. The exercise offers much more promise, in my opinion, than through reasoning alone; working with hauntology and ideal types expanded the potential.

The notion of ideal types as set forth by Weber has been discussed and debated, complicating its definition in ways that are productive for dynamic engagement with the exercise Ghost Images and Ideal Types. Gerhard Wagner and Claudius Härpfer in their essay, "On the Very Idea of an Ideal Type," offer perspectives that have emerged 'in conversation' among diverse disciplinary thinkers, noting that Weber's "conception of the social sciences cannot be adequately understood without embedding it in a broader context that includes the natural sciences as well as aesthetics" (Härpfer, Wagner 2014, p. 230). Weber emphasized that an ideal type is a mental image that one has to sketch or draw (Weber 2012, as cited in Härpfer, Wagner 2014, p. 229). Wager and Härpfer, in their discussion of ideal types, highlight contributions from the 19th-century physiologist and physicist Hermann Helmholtz who distinguished 'logical induction' from 'aesthetic induction,' the latter he claimed was a kind of inference necessary for 'complicated' cases (Helmholtz 1995 [1862], as cited in Härpfer, Wagner 2014, pp. 226, 227).

> According to Helmholtz, it is an essential part of an artist's talent to reproduce by words, by form and colour, or by tones the external indications of a character or a state of mind, and by a kind of "intuitive intuition" to grasp the necessary steps by which we pass from one mood to another: "the works of great artists bring before us characters and moods with such a lifelikeness, with such a wealth of individual traits and such an overwhelming conviction of truth, that they almost seem to be more real than the reality itself, because all disturbing influences are eliminated."
>
> (Helmholtz 1995, p. 85 [1903, p. 172], cited in Härpfer, Wagner 2014, p. 227).

An ideal type is not to be confused with a 'persona'—a fictional composite character that reflects a set of common attributes representing a particular group of people, or 'users' in the case of design thinking tactics in the service of customer-driven activities. The use of personas in design research for social change can be dangerous as such representations might flatten and objectify people. In Weber's terms, ideal types are not fixed but can grow and be used in different ways in respect to local knowledge and complex personhood (Gordon 2008). Avery Gordon defines complex personhood as:

> the stories people tell about themselves, about their troubles, about their social worlds, and about their society's problems are entangled and weave between what is immediately available as a story and what their imaginations are reaching toward.
>
> (Gordon 2008, p. 4)

Exercising care and compassionate optimism within efforts of collective imagination is critical for shaping unfettered narratives as 'images of change.' At the same time, it is equally important to embrace aesthetics.

Cinema can offer many models as ways of working with Ghost Images and Ideal Types through aesthetics. The opening scene from the film *Velvet Goldmine* by Todd Haynes is one example that I have used when introducing the overall concept and components of the exercise. *Velvet Goldmine* is a fiction feature-length film predominantly set in the 1970s glam rock era of London, while the film also reaches backward and forward from this period (Haynes 1998). Borrowing from the lives of historical figures (Oscar Wilde, David Bowie, Iggy Pop, among others), *Velvet Goldmine* takes liberties in weaving interpersonal and causal relationships in the service of a thesis encompassing issues of gender nonconformity, sexual fluidity, idolatry, ambition, artistic integrity, subcultural movements, and shapeshifting identity. The opening sequence of *Velvet Goldmine* might be examined as a highly aestheticized example of Ghost Images and Ideal Types, cinematically sketching movements across the various nodes anchored by 'images of crisis' and 'images of change.'

> A field of stars in a black sky. A shooting star crosses the frame, ethereal music mixes with fragments of voices from early radio transmissions that fade up between static noises. The view floats downward through clouds, voiceover: "Histories like ancient ruins are the fictions of empires. While everything forgotten hangs in the dark dreams of the past, ever threatening to return." A spaceship zooms past, music swells, clouds part to reveal a cityscape. The frame drifts down past rooftops and closer to a doorstep where an infant lay wrapped in a blanket, a woman from the house in a maid's uniform discovers the baby, a title overlays the image: Dublin 1854. The woman calls out, "Madame Wilde, Richard, come quickly." A man joins her and they inspect the infant to see an emerald broach pinned to their clothes. Dissolve: children in an elementary school classroom, they stand one at a time and recite: "I want to be a farmer. I want to be a banister. I want to be a

truckdriver. I want to be a pop idol." Title over black: "One hundred years later …" Overhead wide: a group of schoolboys beating one boy. Close-up: the victim's face against the ground. He finds the same emerald broach. Voiceover: "Childhood, adults always say, is the happiest time in life." Dissolve to, wide tableau: the boy in a hyper-stylized, idyllic, wooded setting strolls along a path toward a low, radiant sun. Voiceover: "But as long as he could remember, Jack Fairy knew better." Medium close-up: the boy illuminated in blue light moves through a dark room, voiceover: "Until one mysterious day when Jack would discover that somewhere there were others, quite like him, singled out for a great gift." Extra close-up: the boy touches the blood on his lip and smears it as though applying lipstick. Portrait: the boy smiling with red lips, looking directly into the camera, voiceover: "And one day the whole stinking world would be theirs."

(Haynes 1998)

Velvet Goldmine is a film about image. The narrative leverages story elements to illuminate a myriad of ways that power and trauma might be transferred across time, generations, social and economic status, and subcultures and the ways this might be performed, communicated, translated, reconceptualized, renegotiated, repositioned, instrumentalized, and so on. Cinematic tropes rely on affective aesthetics to render mood as motivations for character and plot progressions. How might efforts to change one's own or someone else's mood, mind, or perspectives be a gesture of activism? Haynes, in *Velvet Goldmine*, homes in on and teases the complicated nature of these kinds of efforts through an exchange between characters Curt Wild, a retired pop idol, and Arthur Stuart, a fanboy turned investigative journalist,

Curt Wild: "A real artist creates beautiful things and … puts nothing of his own life into them. Okay?" Arthur Stuart: "Is that what you did?" Curt Wild: "No. No. We set out to change the world and ended up … just changing ourselves." Arthur Stuart: "What's wrong with that?" Curt Wild: "Nothing … If you don't look at the world."

(Haynes 1998)

How might image-oriented narratives support design researchers to be more fearlessly open to the full spectrum of humanity across a myriad of temporal contexts and forms in their investigative, reflective, and imaginative practices? How might design researchers, while exercising great care and ethical consideration, approach 'image of crisis' and 'image of change' frameworks in ways that allow for processes to relish complicated and contested situations as they might emerge, rather than predetermining the mood, scope, stakeholder profiles, and possible outcomes? 'Cinematic Tropes as Design Process,' a course that I developed and teach at The New School, uses narratology and the language of cinema as a way to experiment with aesthetic affect—form—for addressing issues—content—within design research processes. In addition to film screenings and seminars, the course focuses on several assignments using the exercise Ghost Images and Ideal Types. I have also introduced the exercise to students and faculty from across the university, as well as to corporate executives, community leaders, and other practitioners around the world.

Let's return to the example where the 'cause' for the 'problem' of cancer was cited as a failure of urban policy and lack of concern for public health. In this scenario, the way forward resides in the potential for the design of new policy—the 'opportunity' (wedge #6 of the diagram), and this opportunity is leveraged through a deeper understanding of the 'source' (wedge #5 of the diagram)—the particular context of urban planning and policy-making. By refining and operationalizing opportunities at hand, in this case, the detailed urban planning policies and public health programs, 'solutions' (wedge #7 of the diagram), are created. The 'image of change' (wedge #8 in the diagram), in this scenario, is the healthy body. Change, rather than being the cure for cancer, would be that the incidence of cancer has been dramatically reduced by altering the conditions of 'cause' and 'threat.' The 'image of change' is not simply a representation of a positive outcome, but rather a thickly rendered prefigurative gesture. In this way, the 'image of change' functions as a model, vividly illustrating what might emerge as transformed, perhaps through the transcendence of collective effervescence, and ideally toward collective liberation. Designing an 'image of change' for the example exercise focused on cancer could be prompted by the question: How might this particular community comprise healthier people? Health as a community priority is different from a medical cure for cancer. Ghost Images and Ideal Types works to evolve more inclusive ways of seeing the nuanced configurations of people's lives which are often illegible and obscured by the hyper-legibility of 'pain points'—the more traditional, and often dangerously reductive, design approach for identifying problems and designing solutions.

Ghost Images and Ideal Types might not be the most elegant name for a design research exercise, while part of my intention was for this particular process to move away from approaches of reasoning as linear or formulaic processes. The exercise, as I have evolved it, supports an elliptical, iterative process for analysis and synthesis informed by and spurring ongoing research and design activities. Graphical representations of the exercise template for Ghost Images and Ideal Types might be rendered best as three-dimensional models that allow for slippages and juxtapositions in motion. Hannah DeVries illustrated a template with wedges of different sizes, simulating the perspective view

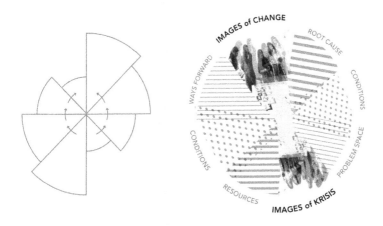

Figure 1.2 Graphic templates for Ghost Images and Ideal Types, by Hannah DeVries (left), and John A. Bruce (right), 2020.

over a spiral staircase. I illustrated a template with overlapping nodal spaces and named the wedges: (1) root cause, (2) conditions, (3) problem space, (4) images of krisis, (5) resources, (6) conditions, (7) ways forward, and (8) images of change. These template ideas invite considerations for dynamic interplay among nodal characteristics, as shown in Figure 1.2.

The exercise is not a device for scripting blueprints that map exact causalities as equations. Despite the arrangement of wedges in a pie diagram numbered from one to eight, the work is never precisely ordered, cleanly categorized, or complete in a single diagram. The exercise provokes questions which invite iterative investigations through participation with people, places, and things in the world. Through the use of the frameworks 'images of crisis' and 'images of change' to analyze and synthesize findings, research agendas can be carried out through greater attunement with situated knowledges and with more respect for the diversity and nuanced perspectives of people's lived experiences in ways central to collective efforts toward transformations.

Practicing with ghost images and ideal types

Working with 'images of crisis' and 'images of change'—constructing, deconstructing, and reconstructing scenarios through representations from field recordings or fictional renderings—can bring issues into focus and also celebrate their poetic resonance and divergent possibilities. Stakeholders, interlocutors, researchers, designers, artists, activists, bystanders, and other *careholders*, nearly everyone has the capacity and, perhaps more importantly, the capability of feeling, to recollect, co-create, and relate to the elements of a cinematic scene. Participation is usually easy, lively, and wildly productive. This experiential framework (as I continue to resist calling it a 'tool') is versatile and can be used to address any area of inquiry and applied to almost any situational context and scale.

At Parsons School of Design, I have been working with students and using Ghost Images and Ideal Types as part of design research processes in a number of different courses. In particular, a project titled Hum, created by Javiera Arenas, Rachel Murray, and Ankita Roy, showcases the productive insights gleaned through rendering 'images of crisis' and 'images of change' within phases of investigation and design development. Hum originated as project work within the studio "Design for Living and Dying," as part of the Transdisciplinary Design MFA program, and, according to the research team, "is an experience designed to create moments between patients and their core circle of caregivers through the engagement in meaningful activities together" (Arenas et al. 2017). The research focused on questions addressing how families might identify and build capacities for coping with terminal illness as it impacts the rhythms of being together and how relationships might evolve in ways that serve the needs of reconfigured care dynamics within friend and family circles. Investigations utilized fiction filmmaking techniques to render 'images of crisis' by at first drafting several versions of a shooting script, eventually workshopped and rehearsed with New York City stage actors. One of the student designers, Ankita Roy, also participated in the scene, playing the role of the daughter alongside actors playing a mother, father, and son. Roy, participating in the writing and acting of the dramatic performances, gained insights that were exceptionally attuned having been gleaned through embodied learning. Writing, rehearsing, directing, acting, and editing the scene served as a uniquely fertile sandbox for the design team and their interlocutors. From the Hum design brief:

> We started our process in developing what would later become Hum by using film as an ethnographic method to zoom in and understand the story of one family dealing with a crisis. Our goal was to explore a crisis within a family unit and illustrate multiple perspectives from stakeholders. We explored 4 key areas: Contrasts of Forces (different coping mechanisms like controlling the situation or expressing anger), Family Ruptures (uncertainty leading to avoiding important conversations), Lack of Safe Space (environmental influence on

nervousness), and Rituals of Intensification (varied approaches to addressing illness, like the cultural promotion of a "fight" mentality as the 'right' approach).

(Arenas et al. 2017)

The design team produced a pair of short companion films illuminating an 'image of crisis' and an 'image of change'; still frames from the videos appear in Figure 1.3. In the first film, a family sits around a café table having just received news from the mother that the illness she has been challenged by is without cure and will cause the end of her life, while in the short term she can lead an otherwise normal existence. The scene plays out in mostly silent glances and nuanced emotive gestures that speak volumes, indicating states of awkward paralysis that prevent any kind of exchange among the family members that might honestly address the issues of mortality at hand. The embodied tensions that fill the air are palpable and invite viewers to explore the moment free from didactic information. The narrative does not explain the situation and rather reveals the complex dynamics of perspectives and roles of the relationships within a particular context. Time and space are uniquely inhabited as illuminated through the mise-en-scéne of the video. The crisis comes into focus with an expanded richness of information and without being overshadowed by the 'problem' of a terminal illness. One key leverage point—the place to potentially intervene in this particular system—focuses on capacities to engage in meaningful exchanges while confronting destabilizing conditions.

The process revealed several salient leverage points that would direct the design team toward refined research agendas and eventually design principles that focused their proposal, Hum—a set of exercises supported by assets including prompts for reigniting rituals among family members, as

Figure 1.3 Still images from research videos exploring 'images of crisis' and 'images of change,' with Ankita Roy seated on the right in frames one and two, for the development of the design project Hum, by Javiera Arenas, Rachel Murray, and Ankita Roy, 2017.

Figure 1.4 Hum exercises, by Javiera Arenas, Rachel Murray, and Ankita Roy, 2017.

shown in Figure 1.4. The trust and camaraderie developed during the many stages of filmmaking and role-play supported a rigorous and joyous development process that informed Hum's content and form.

Let's return to the six-and-a-half-minute video of Ram Dass to understand this artifact in relation to Ghost Images and Ideal Types. The 'image of crisis' is an old white man with a bandage on his nose, staring at you, about to say something, yet he doesn't speak. As minutes of strange stillness go by, our expectation of cinema—action and dialogue unfolding to provide information—is betrayed. For some who encounter this video, the 'problem' is being uncomfortable with uncertainty and mystery, and also perhaps the anxiety that often accompanies awkward anticipation. We might speculate that the conditions present for such a problem to arise—the 'threats'—are the strong assumptions that information can be readily accessed everywhere and at any and all times. A possible 'cause' for such conditions: addiction to instant gratification as accelerated by social media. These notions are not theories or conclusions and are rather points of departure for further explorations. The exercise Ghost Images and Ideal Types is designed to facilitate multi-stakeholder discursive exchanges through images and narratives and potentially spur co-creative image-oriented expressions for nondiscursive exchanges and embodied learning.

The frameworks for working with 'images of crisis' and 'images of change' engage narratology to support modes of learning through making within participatory research and design processes. These perspectives and practices can help build capacities for scholars and practitioners within transdisciplinary approaches that contribute in significant ways to exploratory social sciences and humanities. In Chapter 2 of this book, 'Proximity and Duration, Senses and Images,' a closer examination of aesthetics for working with image-oriented narrative is discussed. Chapter 3, 'Movement and Thresholds,' discusses theories of organization and systems dynamics in relation to the use of narrative to transgress boundaries that otherwise inhibit collaborative actions toward collective liberation. Chapter 4 of this book, 'Cinematic Tropes and Designing Spectacles,' further explores notions of 'images of change' as prefigurative design gestures in the service of transformations for a more environmentally and socially just future. While employing stories to raise awareness is useful, systemic change also demands being and working together, as "the task of resistance movements will not be to provoke, but rather to create (coextensively with the insurrection) autonomous structures for knowledge, existence, survival," as Franco Bifo Berardi states in his book *The Uprising: On Poetry and Finance* (Berardi 2012, p. 49).

Image-oriented narratives rendered like scenes from a movie and responding to notions of crisis and change are familiar and accessible entry points for participatory research and design—ways to get closer, by proxy, to people and things—*be with them*. These are not didactic or prescriptive formulas for design, as the crisis is not always a broken place and change is not always desirable for all things and people. Design processes working with images and narratives in these ways can illuminate the cracks within seemingly impenetrable and unmovable situations where social transformations are desired for healthier and more just futures. Participation in sustainable ways forward begins with embodied learning for new ways of knowing—thoughts and action embracing the opportunities in a moment of *krisis*, as in the Greek word krīnō, 'I decide'. The complicated nature of deciding invites participation through approaches of design.

References

Arenas, J., Murray, R., Roy, A. (2017) *Hum* [experience design and research videos]. Retrieved from www.designforlivinganddying.com.

Berardi, F. (2012) *The Uprising: On Poetry and Finance*, Los Angeles, CA: Semiotext(e).

Berardi, F. (2017) "Is There a Way Out?" e-flux lecture event, March 20, 2017, New York, NY. Available at https://www.e-flux.com/announcements/121730/e-flux-lecture-series/

Bruce, J.A., Wojtasik, P. (Directors) (2017) *End of Life*, US: Grasshopper Films.

Bruce, J.A., Wojtasik, P. (Directors) (2017) *End of Life*, US: Grasshopper Films. Reflection Exercise excerpt, Retrieved from https://vimeo.com/269308911.

Bruun, H.H., (2016) *Science, Values and Politics in Max Weber's Methodology: New Expanded Edition (Rethinking Classical Sociology)*, Burligton, VT: Ashgate Publishing Company.

Didion, J. (1979) *The White Album*, New York: Simon and Schuster.

Freedom Lab (2007) *Wheel of Reasoning* [illustration]. Retrieved from freedomlab.org.

Gordon, A. (2008) *Ghostly Matters: Haunting and the Sociological Imagination*, Minneapolis: University of Minnesota Press.

Grace, B. (2007) *Change Agent in Residence* [Lecture to the Opening Circle], at The Bainbridge Graduate Institute, Bainbridge Island, October.

Guibert, H. (2014 [1982]) *Ghost Image*, trans. R. Bononno, Chicago: The University of Chicago Press.

Halberstam, J. (2011) *The Queer Art of Failure*, Durham: Duke University Press.

Harris, H. (2020) *How Steve McQueen Pulled Off the Year's Best Movie Scene*, New York Magazine, November 17.

Haynes, T. (Director) (1998) *Velvet Goldmine*, London, UK: FilmFour Distribution; New York, US: Miramax Films.

Helmholtz, H. von (1903 [1862]) Ueber das Verhältniss der Naturwissenschaften zur Gesammtheit der Wissenschaft: Akademische Festrede gehalten zu Heidelberg beim Antritt des Prorectorats 1862. In Hermann von Helmholtz, ed. *Vorträge und Reden*. 5th ed., Vol. 1. Braunschweig: Friedrich Vieweg und Sohn, pp. 157–185.

Helmholtz, H. von (1995 [1862]) On the Relation of Natural Science to Science in General. In David Cahan, ed. *Hermann von Helmholtz, Science and Culture: Popular and Philosophical Essays*. Chicago: University of Chicago Press.

Hunt, J. (2010) Prototyping the Social: Temporality and Speculative Futures at the Intersection of Design and Culture. In Alison Clark, ed. *Design Anthropology: Object Culture in the 21st Century*. New York: Springer, p. 35.

Ison, R. (2018) Transdisciplinarity as transformation: a cybersystemic thinking in practice perspective. In D. Fam, J. Palmer, C. Riedy, C. Michell, eds. *Transdisciplinary Research and Practice for Sustainability Outcomes*, London: Routledge, Taylor & Francis Group, Earthscan from Routledge, pp. 55–73.

Klein, J.T. (2018) Transdisciplinarity and Sustainability: Patterns of Definition. In D. Fam, J. Palmer, C. Riedy, C. Mitchell, eds. *Transdisciplinary Research and Practice for Sustainability Outcomes*, London: Routledge, Taylor & Francis Group, Earthscan from Routledge, pp. 7–21.

Koestler, A. (1967) *The Ghost in the Machine*, London: Hutchinson.

Lawrence, R.J. (2018) Future directions: a trans-anthropo-logic of transdisciplinarity. In D. Fam, J. Palmer, C. Riedy, C. Michell, eds. *Transdisciplinary Research and Practice for Sustainability Outcomes*, London: Routledge, Taylor & Francis Group, Earthscan from Routledge, pp. 253–259.

McQueen, S. (Director) (2020) *Lovers Rock*, US: Amazon Studios.

Mills, C.W. (2000 [1959]) *The Sociological Imagination*, New York: Oxford University Press.

Mulgan, G. (2021) *The Case for Exploratory Social Sciences*, Hamburg: The New Institute Foundation gGmbH.

Muñoz, J.E. (2019) *Cruising Utopia, 10th Anniversary Edition: The Then and There of Queer Futurity*, New York: New York University Press.

Nicolescu, B. (2007) Transdisciplinarity–Past, Present and Future. In B. Haverkort, C. Reijntjes, eds. *Moving Worldviews: Reshaping Sciences, Policies, and Practices for Endogenous Sustainable Development*, Leusden Compassions, pp. 142–166.

Piaget, J. (1972) L'épistémologie des relations interdisciplinaires, in: *Apostel et al.*

Singh, M. (2021) "The California region where Covid 'just isn't slowing down'," *The Guardian*, Wednesday September 29, 2021.

trans (2010) Oxford Dictionary of English, 2nd ed., Oxford, England: Oxford University Press.

Villegas, P. (2020) South Dakota Nurse Says Many Patients Deny the Coronavirus Exists— Right up Until Death. *The Washington Post.*

Weber, M. (1959) *The Methodology of the Social Sciences*, translation Edward A. Shils and Henry A. Finch, New York: The Free Press.

Weber, M. (2012) *Collected Methodological Writings*, eds. Hans Henrik Bruun and Sam Whimster; translation Hans Henrik Bruun, London: Routledge.

Wittgenstein, L. (1922) *Tractatus Logico-Pbilosophicus*. Trans. C. K. Ogden. London: Routledge and Kegan Paul.

2 Proximity and duration, senses and images

"This book I'm working on is going to be a wowzer. It's very beautiful, if I do say so. And then I'm on to the next one. There's always more and more and more. Which is lucky." These are the first statements we hear from Sarah Grossman in *End of Life*, a nonfiction film informed through participatory research with five people in the process of dying (Bruce, Wojtasik 2017). Sarah Grossman was an activist and author of children's books. She spent the last three years of her life in a nursing home after a stroke had left her body almost completely paralyzed. Although she was nearly 90 years old, bedridden, and frail, Sarah did not suffer from dementia, but rather persisted very strategically through exerting her imaginative energies to regale visitors with elaborate narratives. She would sometimes weave bedside audiences into her stories that blended fiction and nonfiction in nonlinear time. The medium close-up image of Sarah Grossman, as shown in Figure 2.1, was rendered by a camera positioned along the side of and at the same height as her bed, directly receiving her gaze. The camera, a small DSLR, was mounted on a monopod, requiring support by an operator, in this case, me—kneeling next to the bed with my head very close to the lens. During the recording session, Sarah addressed me, while the recorded image performs her gaze to the viewers of the film. The appearance of the image is dominant within a scene which has a duration of 18 minutes, does not utilize any edits, and features only a few minor movements by the camera. The presence of the researchers, Paweł Wojtasik and me, is revealed in the scene through their voices as well as for one moment when the camera moves to see Wojtasik positioned with his camera at the foot of the bed.

Over the course of nearly two years, we collaborated with Sarah Grossman at a rehabilitation and care facility in Brooklyn, New York, where she was a patient. On some days, our visits would last for four or five hours, depending on Sarah's desire and capacity to share her experiences. On other days, we might arrive to find Sarah sleeping and sit quietly for a few hours without ever speaking with her. Our cameras were not always

DOI: 10.4324/9780367365264-2

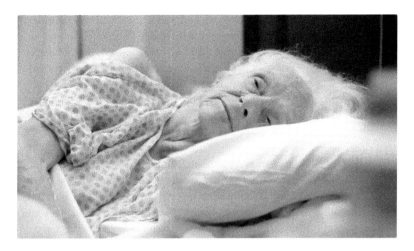

Figure 2.1 Sarah Grossman from the film *End of Life* by John Bruce and Paweł Wojtasik, 2017.

operating and sometimes not even unpacked from their bags. In addition to conversing with Sarah and operating our recording equipment, we were often engaged in activities of care and companionship during our visits— assisting in ways to make her more comfortable, helping with meals, reading letters and books, and watching television together. Sarah could move one of her arms and her head, but nothing else. She could speak clearly and related accounts of her past and present experiences with vivid detail, astute analytical reasoning, and, quite often, brilliant poetic phrasing.

The close-up image of Sarah Grossman (shown in Figure 2.1), as projected on a large screen in a theater, is unrelenting in its command of the viewer's attention. The image, at a cinematic scale, is a wowzer. Sarah's body, although in decline and mostly inert, is revealed through visceral signs of life—eye movements, breathing, pulsations of a vein in her neck— that invite viewers into greater awareness of their own bodies, senses, and mortality. The viewer, forced to sit with this close-up for 18 minutes, is afforded contemplative time and space. The duration of the image allows for encounters with the contingent details of experiences at the end of life that are beyond the surface of the image and illuminate more than merely the events of a plot (Balsom 2007). In this way, contemplative learning takes place through an embodied experience by proxy.

Proximity involves being close to things in space, in time, and through relationships. Cinema exploits the possibilities of proximity and duration.

Cinema as a proxy for lived experiences can provide unique affordances for vision—a dynamic range of focal and audio perspectives, nonlinear time, juxtaposition, montage, mise-en-scène, manipulation of motion, and other modes for expanding the capabilities of human senses. Participatory research and design—being with people, things, and situations—can benefit from cinema and cinematic approaches in a myriad of ways for engaging embodied, co-creative, and multidirectional learning. Addressing complex social issues demands presence within context—sensorial acts of investigation, reflection, translation, and other experimental forms for discursive and nondiscursive exchange.

This chapter explores proximity and duration as potential affective qualities for experiential encounters and for working with image-oriented artifacts within participatory design research processes, specifically in efforts of transformation toward collective liberation. Chapter 3, Movement and Thresholds, continues this discussion by examining notions of sensory experiences entangled with the role of identity formation and acts of identification. The workshop exercise Situated Narratives, presented in this chapter, provides an approach for leveraging cinematic tropes in relation to themes of participatory design discussed throughout this book, and especially in Chapters 2 and 3.

Learning through cinema

Proximity can be understood in terms of 'cinematic scale,' and the two distinct ways this can be made manifest are through "the size of the image itself and the relative proximity or distance from which the image is captured" (Balsom 2007, pp. 25–26). The relationships between image scale and image size within cinematic possibilities are intriguing, complex, and vast. The discussion of cinematic scale in this book serves only as an introduction to these ideas and draws upon the work of film and media scholars Erika Balsom and Mary Ann Doane, among others, as well as from my own practice. Balsom underlines the particular value in the combination of *plan rapproché*—"the shot taken from a great proximity"—and *gros plan*—"the image projected at large scale" (Balsom 2007, p. 26). She quotes Sergei Eisenstein to underscore the power of proximity, "[T]he laws of cinematographic perspective are such that a cockroach filmed in close-up appears as fearsome on the screen as a hundred elephants in long shot" (Eisenstein 1974, p. 229, cited in Balsom 2007, p. 26). Certainly, the experience of viewing images projected on a large screen in a dark room is quite different from watching images on television, laptop, or smartphone screens. The combination of *close-up* qualities—*plan rapproché* and *gros plan*—can imbue images with reverence. Doane writes, "The specter of the close-up is raised whenever an object or person moves toward the camera, potentially putting into crisis the distance between screen and spectator, threatening to bridge the abyss of representation" (Doane 2021, p. 12). Devising ways for working with this space of crisis or 'krisis'—extreme opportunity, as discussed in Chapter 1, Images of Crisis, Images of Change—can provide great learning opportunities for participatory design.

Cinema-goers are captive audiences. In a theater, viewers cannot turn away from images, except by averting their gaze into darkness. Confrontations with images recorded proximately can spur contemplative encounters and invite a reckoning with the expanded essence of objects. A close-up of Sarah's hand becomes more than a part of Sarah's body—it exudes decades of labor, wisdom, the care of caress. At cinematic scale, objects might expand into a grand world unto themselves, even though they are also 'sub-wholes' with a larger system—hands of a body. Images larger than human scale assume dominance in a space and can work to complicate divisions between the subject and the object, for the power of their presence serves to lead the action—commanding attention rather than being passively consumed. The qualities of the duration of such confrontations—the more time one remains present with encounters at cinematic scale and the cinematic manipulations of time—can also expand perspectives for potential sense-making through unique affordances of contemplative learning. Notions concerning cinematic scale raise questions for how participatory design practices might benefit from leveraging proximity and duration as strategies during processes for field recording and for the analysis and synthesis of image-oriented findings.

Chris Marker's seminal film *Sans Soleil* dissolves the divisions of subject and object through strategies of proximity and duration in ways that invite viewers to engage in a kind of self-reflective 'embodied' learning as afforded by cinematic proxy. The images in *Sans Soleil* depict people and places in the style of a travelogue—an assembly of shuffled locations, mostly Japan, along with Guinea-Bissau and Cape Verde islands, Île-de-France, San Francisco, and Iceland. The film evokes an otherworldly distance, despite the proximal relation of the camera to many of its subjects. The scenes exude an aesthetic of a wandering poet and are accompanied by the voice of an anonymous woman, in voiceover, reciting letters written by (as implied) the maker of the images. One sequence proceeds,

He wrote me: I will have spent my life trying to understand the function of remembering, which is not the opposite of forgetting, but rather its lining. We do not remember, we rewrite memory much as history is rewritten. How can one remember thirst?

(Marker 1983)d

These lines are delivered over a series of images with a total duration of about 30 seconds: a mountain range viewed from just above the clouds; a shoreline from a high angle; a medium close-up of the seafoam edge of waves breaking on the sand where a dog reclines; an aerial view of a hilly terrain, and a medium close-up of a person looking at the sea from a moving boat, who turns to glance directly at the camera for an instant and then resumes an outward gaze as the frame freezes—all sound and motion stopping abruptly. The sequence ends with a disruption of movement, of life, that suspends the limits of time, collapses distance, and affords reflection and exchange among filmmaker, images, and viewers. These kinds of cinematic tropes complicate and question notions of seeing, being seen, and acts of 'making seen.' Participatory design relies on these same sensorial practices.

San Soleil works to develop a theme of shifting perspective that is explored throughout the film, and especially during a sequence taking place in a Guinea-Bissau market when the gaze of the camera is countered by the gaze of a woman staring back into the lens, after a prolonged 'exchange,' as the voiceover narrates:

> I see her, she saw me, she knows that I see her, she drops me her glance, but just at an angle where it is still possible to act as though it was not addressed to me, and at the end the real glance, straightforward, that lasted a twenty-fourth of a second, the length of a film frame.
>
> (Marker 1983)

Multidirectional flows of information, rendered through cinematic affordances of proximity, attempt to decentralize the authorship of meaning-making in *San Soleil*, "Part of the meaning ... is the ambiguity of causes, of agency, of direction itself, in the dreams and nightmares of contemporary history—the issue of who is doing what to whom," writes Jonathan Rosenbaum (Rosenbaum 2007). Film scholars have debated the status of *San Soleil* as a documentary, and some have proposed that the film is a critique of documentary in that it is not representational yet gives access to Truth (Casebier 1988, p. 35). *San Soleil* raises critical questions around the distinctions between the affect potential of images—especially those created and experienced through proximal encounters—and the notion of documentary forms as representations of objective truth.

Marker utilizes proximity and duration to render ways of seeing, being seen, and making seen that complicate linear and didactic points of view. In *San Soleil*, images are exploited in ways that detach their appearance from notions of a universal referent, disrupting the expectations for a more traditionally defined narrative—stories that drive a plot through the motivations and actions of people or person-like characters. Exchanges take place among humans and nonhumans that *move*—with regard to agency, efficacy, affect, and impact—in multiple directions. For instance, the film's relationship with cats (real animals and also the well-known statuette of a cat with a waving arm) is aligned with the polytheism of Shinto beliefs that all things possess a soul and divine power.

> He wrote me that in the suburbs of Tokyo there is a temple consecrated to cats. I wish I could convey to you the simplicity – the lack of affectation – of this couple who had come to place an inscribed wooden slat in the cat cemetery so their cat Tora would be protected. No she wasn't dead, only run away. But on the day of her death no one would know how to pray for her, how to intercede with death so that he would call her by her right name. So they had to come there, both of them, under the rain, to perform the rite that would repair the web of time where it had been broken.
>
> (Marker 1983)

Acts of encounter have long been the center of ethnographic practices. Historically, as well as today, ethnographic practices that assume, even unconsciously, colonial and extractive forms or reinforce 'narratives of damage,' as Eve Tuck eloquently addresses in "Suspending Damage: A Letter to Communities," can cause harm (Tuck 2009). Participatory research processes, if they are to be ethically attuned to people and situations, must privilege conditions that support atmospheres where experiences of encounter are multidirectional, rather than positioned to consolidate power as defined by subjective actions. Participatory engagements can be more fulsome and inclusive of situated knowledges, where acts of countering an encounter—reacting to an action, being attracted to, or withdrawing from a seduction—might flourish unfettered and be acknowledged with respect, thoughtfulness, and care. In this argument, I borrow the term 'counter encounter' from the research and curating collective Counter-Encounters, a cinema and art initiative exploring forms of alter- and anti-ethnographies, co-founded by Laura Huertas Millan and Rachael Rakes. Participatory design research activities that are ethnographic and also center expansive notions of 'counter-encounters,' can ideally spur collective effervescence toward collective liberation. These kinds of 'countering acts' are more than the result of provocations and are rather the emergent flow of reciprocal exchanges—gestures of curiosity, care, desire, and other expressions of conjunctive encounter. Conjunction is distinguished from connection, according to Franco Bifo Berardi, in that connecting anticipates ways for things to fit perfectly—coded and predetermined exchanges like certain machines and their operating software, while acts of conjunction are messier, rounder, reflective, and generative, similar to the way that "love changes the lover" (Berardi 2015, p. 18). These notions of counter-encounters echo the opening line of *Ghost Image* by Guibert, "Photography is also an act of love" (Guibert [1982] 2014, p. 10). The encounters of lovers are expressions of desire as recognitions that also reflect back, in both directions. Perhaps the Velvet Underground says it more clearly, "I'll be your mirror" (Reed 1966).

San Soleil is a film about documentary film. Debates concerning the role of documenting as a form of representation have taken place long before *San Soleil* and continue today with ever-increasing complexity. *San Soleil* is cinema as a mode of deconstruction that invites participation for expanded possibilities of sense-making. Marker uses images as an expression of thinking by showing how the visual can be more expressive and articulate than even the strongest prose. In fact, when we position writing as a privileged form, we overlook how writing so often conforms to reductive structures in building convincing arguments.

The voiceover in *San Soleil* accentuates ambiguity in regard to the causality one might expect to glean through documentary and narrative logic. The film's spoken text, while aesthetically pleasing in its ethereal rhythm and tone, works to confuse possible understandings of how and why the images might have been created and how they might function for the viewer, rather than adding clarifications. The uncertainties proliferate rather than diminish. The narrator is indeed unreliable and without any substantiated authority other than having been designated to read the letters from a fictitious author, Sandor Krasna, who is disembodied and presented without any context of origin, destination, or ultimate objective for these travels and the resultant images. Marker is behind Krasna's camera (is Krasna?), but why such a transparent disguise? In the opening sequence of the film, Marker tips his hand—the voiceover describes the images from a filmmaker's perspective:

> The first image he told me about was of three children on a road in Iceland, in 1965. He said that for him it was the image of happiness and also that he had tried several times to link it to other images, but it never worked. He wrote me: one day I'll have to put it all alone at the beginning of a film with a long piece of black leader; if they don't see happiness in the picture, at least they'll see the black.
>
> (Marker 1983)

Do the fragmented perspectives belong to Krasna or to a collective memory or dream? *San Soleil* is an example of a visualization strategy in that it manipulates the idea of what might be seen—images appear while the viewer's attention is intentionally misdirected by the voiceover in ways that undermine the subjectivity of the camera. The film refuses for Marker or the camera to be the reliable source of any *god trick* of objective vision. In this way, *San Soleil* strives to decentralize authorship, inviting diversified perspectives to grapple with questions of sense-making.

Sarah Grossman, as a source of telling and showing stories in the film *End of Life*, complicates subject–object relationships, while she is, unlike Sandor Krasna and his reader of letters, a reliable narrator. She speaks directly and powerfully to the camera. Sarah's performance, through strategies of cinematic scale and duration, decentralizes authorship in a unique way. The researchers, people farther from the end of their lives, approach Sarah, who is closer to dying, through a participatory process that invites conditions for counter-encounters. The proximal distance of the cameras and researchers to Sarah serves to 'bridge the abyss of representation'—an 'image of crisis'—in ways that provoke reverberating shifts in the 'points-of-view'—who is doing what to whom—among the image, the image-makers, and the image perceivers (Doane 2021; Suchman 2002). During the 18-minute scene, Sarah recalls the lyrics to a song and begins to sing, which leads to the swell of her emotions and infuses her singing with wailing cries. Following this moment, the scene continues, without edits, and as Sarah quickly regains a calm composure, she looks into the lens and says,

A couple of days before the dreadful accident, the children came into my bedroom, and the little boy said to his sister, 'remember, we run up to the bed laughing,' he said. He had a sense of drama. To run up to my bed laughing is quite different from just running up to my bed. They seemed to have a keen appreciation of … the need for drama … of the good sort. Because some children could have thought it was a burden to go see the old lady. But they didn't think that.

(Bruce, Wojtasik 2017)

Confronting this moment—this image—in the cinema was reported as unnerving for some audience members—*unable to turn away*, having experienced the scene as both *plan rapproché* and *gros plan*. It is immersive and visceral. Several viewers who encountered the film on a laptop instead of in a cinema setting reported that they had stopped watching the film after the sequence during which Sarah sings, cries, and shares the story about children 'running up to my bed.' The film presents Sarah's image as both performance and reflection by Sarah through her direct actions and reactions to the audience and thus collapses the distances of representation and the divisions of subject and object. Perhaps the viewers who switched off the film could not accept Sarah's agency and efficacy in 'telling' her own story of mortality—immanently evolving—as delivered through acts of showing intentionally aimed at the film audience, and thus rejected her acts of countering their encounter. They were caught looking. Did this, perhaps, raise a sense of accountability for these viewers? And, if so, was this sense of accountability in response to Sarah, to their consciousness of their own mortality, or to both? The discomfort that can arise from such a confrontation might provoke the assumption that the camera and the researchers are violating Sarah's privacy and that the viewer is also complicit, by proxy, in this violation. By rejecting Sarah's performance, viewers might be seeking comfort in perspectives that conflate notions of privacy with self-protective acts of separating oneself from mortality—a kind of distancing that can marginalize the dying person. In the film *End of Life*, Sarah performs her role as an activist and author, as well as very consciously serving as a collaborator within participatory design research. She is participating in the 'invitation of design' through her proximity to the camera and the duration of her shared expressions. Her son is a celebrated documentary filmmaker, and her first husband was a well-known documentary photographer. While I was present with Sarah Grossman, she often reached out and touched my camera and said, "Voitlander," naming the brand of lens. During Sarah's penultimate appearance in *End of Life*, as she was moving closer to active dying, she says,

> Creating this kept me from insanity in the nursing home. Believe me, it isn't nursing and it isn't home. … You should think about it before it overtakes you, and suddenly you have to go into a place that you haven't examined. … So, act before suddenly there you are, you're 75, and you have no place to go, sort of. If you look ahead, you can avoid that. For rich people, it's no problem. But for your type, it will be quite a difficulty. You have to go in, in the morning at breakfast time, and stay the day. And see what they do, whether they actually encourage creative activity or whether that's just catalogue talk, you know? Being in the middle of it, I can't tell you strongly enough that you and your pets and your children have to be welcome there. Thank you for your help.
>
> (Bruce, Wojtasik 2017)

Navigating relationships with the collaborators of the *End of Life* project demanded open and iterative dialogue for addressing a myriad of ethical questions, personal parameters, and preferences for modes of participation. These considerations include consent in the most expanded sense, as consent is certainly never limited to only a form or singular statement for granting access. Our conversations with the five people experiencing the end of life in our project, *End of Life*, made clear that the research process would focus on experiences as they unfolded in ways open to emergence while contingent on their ongoing consent. These conversations included discussions about non-preconception—perspectives on dying were not assumed in advance, and there were no specific expectations for a film that might result from the research. There were no preconceived points or agendas that we, the researchers and filmmakers, were setting out to argue or achieve in regard to certain positions concerning the medical and care industries or any other relational or institutional dynamic surrounding the end of life. We maintained a position of being open to whatever might happen or not happen, whatever might be said or not said, without any specified criteria for acts of sharing, explaining, or identifying. We set one key guiding principle for our process: the focus of our participation would be limited to our presence with the dying person. We chose to abstain from pursuing other potential elements of a narrative ecosystem—interviews with experts, establishing shots, or other expositional devices—and instead focused our process of participation as dedicated to experiences that embraced proximity and duration. In this way, we expressed our preference for recording participatory behavior over any kind of simplifying didactic representation. This approach was maintained through our mediation during the editing process of the film—we avoided using montage as a heavy-handed meaning-making device (while any act of assembling images cannot completely escape some degree of imposing meaning) and did not use any intertitles or 'lower third' lines of text for identifying people, places, or situations. Nor did we employ any music, as is rather often the case where cinema attempts to cue and direct emotional responses.

Consent emerges from relationships and must be approached in the light of the complexity of people's lives within the shifting circumstances that surround processes for sharing information and co-creating images and narratives. Consent requires ongoing, careful, and rigorous exchanges to support conditions for mutual understanding and agreement. These exchanges can be richly creative, informative, and integral to the process and are not merely administrative details. Participatory design research processes, if they strive to decentralize authorship and expand persistence of vision, must privilege a commitment to relationships as the basis for experiences. This is true whether or not image-making serves as central to the process. Notions of proximity and duration can help to guide the activities within these relationships. Participatory design processes benefit through centering relationships as an ethical compass, and thus, forms of encounter, reflection, and critique must embrace the complexity by which activities traverse and reverberate among matters of fact and concern (Latour 2004). Relationships in terms of consent are also a matter of care.

Reading traces and sculpting in time

"Zoom out," is an instruction, or piece of advice, commonly delivered when meaning-making capacities become stuck—trapped in assumptions or restricted by the narrow view of a situation. Design practices for addressing complex ecosystems are often charged with exercises for 'zooming out' and 'zooming in'—ways to perceive a situation at various scales and scope. Design education has long relied on the film by Charles and Ray Eames, *Powers of Ten*, as a poetic illustration of seeing systems through shifting viewpoints of scale (Eames 1977). Shifts in proximal viewpoints—'zooming in' and 'zooming out'—to see whole systems and their elements might be understood, in a simplistic sense, by the examples of pointillism painting (as in the work of George Seurat) or four-color printing—many small dots of color that rely on the viewer's eye and mind to mix the dots into one, larger cohesive image. Viewing a pointillist painting in close-up reveals only the dots—'sub-wholes' of the system—while the bigger picture can only be understood by stepping back from the surface. There is a great deal to consider in regard to *movement* and gleaning perspectives, as discussed in Chapter 3, Movement and Threshold.

Acts of 'zooming in' and 'zooming out' with the aid of image-oriented artifacts, such as the exercise Ghost Images and Ideal Types, as discussed in Chapter 1, Images or Crisis, Images of Change, are more than merely ways of seeing images and are modes of visuality and visualization. Nicholas Mirzoeff writes, "to visualize is not to make visible but to suspect what can be seen and to manipulate it" (Mirzoeff 2011, p. 1192). Mirzoeff suggests that "the image is deployed within a regime of visualization, whose success or failure accounts for its reception" (Mirzoeff 2011, p. 1187). Sensing the flow of events and history is often the task of leaders: "'Visuality' is the name for that process by which certain persons claim the authority to determine what may or may not be 'seen,' literally and metaphorically, in the operations of power" (Mirzoeff 2011, p. 1189). *Pay no attention to that man behind the curtain!* Mirzoeff points to counterinsurgency and political narratives where "visualization and the resulting visuality has been a required military tactic when confronted with a battlefield (or 'Area of Operations' in modern parlance) too extensive to be seen by any one individual" (Mirzoeff 2011, p. 1187). A key question arises in regard to visuality as central to operations of power: How might activities contributing to visualization be genuinely inclusive and transparent among participating stakeholders? Collective participation among stakeholders for ordering images as an approach to visualization is perhaps complicated to facilitate, while tenable and also extremely powerful, as discussed later in the exercise Situated Narratives.

Visualization is also the central task of the cinema-maker as auteur. However, I propose that participatory, and especially transdisciplinary, research can benefit from co-opting the visualization strategies of traditional power-holder models through decentralizing the authorship of sense-making activities. Participatory synthesis of research findings can yield potent insights when gleaned from the perspectives of multiple stakeholders as they interact with—confront, manipulate, and order—image-oriented narrative elements. These activities of visualization are especially fruitful when artifacts leverage strategies of proximity and duration and invite messy, generative, discursive, and nondiscursive exchanges. One exercise that I have developed, Situated Narratives, experiments with these process elements and facilitated approaches. A discussion of the exercise is below, and an example of the exercise appears at the end of this chapter.

The affective qualities of narrative are often charged by proximal conditions experienced as duration—a quality of time that is continuous and mobile. Duration is, according to Gilles Deleuze, "consciousness and freedom because it is primarily memory" and is not measurable in units, for a continuum is more than a series of successive moments, and, as eloquently framed by Henri Bergson, "we are not dealing with these moments themselves, since they have vanished forever, but with the lasting traces which they seem to have left in space on their passage through it" (Deleuze 1991, p. 51; Bergson 2001, p. 79).

This notion of 'reading traces' builds upon the discussion of ghost images and haunting, introduced in Chapter 1, Images of Crisis, Images of Change, in that participatory design research can surface and analyze potentially significant qualitative data as revealed through conditions of immanence, anticipation, and emergence; remarkable evidence that is often difficult, if not impossible, to measure quantitatively.

The duration of engagement with an image can profoundly impact perspectives for meaning-making. Experiencing the recorded moving image of a cup of coffee for three seconds can provoke a very different set of understandings as compared to 30 seconds of the same image. What we think we know about the cup of coffee becomes destabilized through the duration of the image—cracks in certainty form and open spaces for a new vision. The space to consider greater perspectives, explore conjunctive possibilities, and revisit memories is afforded through time. The 18-minute scene (one contiguous shot) with Sarah Grossman in *End of Life* is one example of affective durational strategy. The six-and-a-half-minute video of Ram Dass described and discussed in Chapter 1, Images of Crisis, Images of Change, is another example of a durational image-oriented encounter that can be useful as a model for expanding sensibilities within design research processes. The perception of an old white man with a bandage on his nose, seemingly about to say something, can trigger one set of assumptions, while being with this image for an extended period of time expands the capacity of the viewer to imagine a myriad of possible narrative scenarios.

Duration as a narrative strategy might also be experienced as Kairos, supreme time, and beyond the temporality of clock-time—Chronos. Cinematic manipulations of clock-time are commonly manifest through flashbacks and flashforwards—alternative temporal moments juxtaposed with a particular current state moment. Time travel, another device that relies on Chronos, has been used by many films—*Back to the Future, La Jetée, Primer, Groundhog Day, Planet of the Apes, Celine and Julie Go Boating*, and many more. These cinematic strategies remain rooted in Chronos. Kairos—supreme time, or opportunity time—is not contingent on the forward progression of measurable units that define Chronos. It might be useful to revisit the idea of *krisis*, as discussed in Chapter 1, Images of Crisis, Images of Change, in relation to Kairos, especially within the context of the exercise Ghost Images and Ideal Types. The 'image of crisis' or *krisis* is a representative real-time moment, a scene, situated within a fluidly relational schema of the past, present, and future—a composite image or palimpsest rather than a sequence as marked against sequential time. Ghost images, as understood through gestures of hauntology, appear as strategies to complicate time within agendas for provoking attention and action. Ghost images might be considered as agents for queering or hacking Chronos and Kairos—pirates of time (Halberstam 2011). Duration is also worth considering in regard to the terms 'endure' and 'durable' that share their origin from Latin *durare* 'to last' and *durus* 'hard' (*duration* 2010). Like ghost images, the concept of *durational* might refer to that which lasts, suffers, and remains in existence—relationships that endure.

One of the most striking cinematic examples of durational strategies in regard to the idea of 'ghost images' is the film *Transit* by Christian Petzold. Instead of using flashback and flashforward devices, *Transit* slips across and beyond temporal moors by hinting at different periods simultaneously—a layering of referential codes. The fiction film is based on the 1944 novel, of the same name, by Anna Seghers, and follows the movements of a German political refugee who flees an occupied Paris, in the present (Petzold 2018). All the while, the mise-en-scéne of the film mixes elements that evoke both the styles of 1940s and contemporary France. In addition to these aesthetic codes, the behaviors of the characters at certain moments also harken from past cultural mannerisms, albeit rendered with the utmost subtlety. The plot is thick with objectives and stakes that drive the action—mistaken identity, impersonation, illnesses, suicides, romantic intrigues, and urgent quests to seek passage to flee Marseille—while these machinations are merely gestures that trace the contours of larger and timeless themes. *Transit* uses ghost images through expanded notions of duration to surface the quandary of making individual choices toward collective accountabilities while confronting oppressive forces, in this case, fascist totalitarianism. Duration, in the case of *Transit*, functions in tandem with affective qualities of proximity. Today, we, as viewers of the film, can be viscerally engaged in the philosophical quandaries presented in *Transit* afforded through an aesthetic that conjures Kairos.

Visualization strategies utilizing duration might be understood through the notion of the 'recollection-image'—an image-oriented reflection for sense-making that occurs while engaged with moving images. The recollection-image is a virtual image that "forms a circuit with" an actual image— in that "they [recollection-images] insert themselves between stimulation and response" (Deleuze drawing from Bergson [1985] 1989, p. 47). The viewer's response to what they see and hear in the recorded moving image is manifest as a virtual image within subjective sense-making. The 'recollection-image' reverberates within the cinematic experience—blurring the boundary between roles of observation and participation of the viewer— weaving temporal and spiritual senses of subjectivity among the narrative *events*, the *movement*, of the moving images. Time might assume different characteristics of scale and non-sequential ordering—Kairos—as navigated through iterative dialectics of recollection-image responses to images. Slowing down the action (delaying plot progression), slowing down the movement of the images (rendering slow-motion), or freezing the frame (creating a still image) can generate space for the recollection-image to linger and expand. In this way, the viewer's meaning-making process is afforded generative time and space.

The film *End of Life* also relies on an aesthetics of Kairos in that distances are collapsed between the filmmakers who are farther from the end of life and the characters in the film who are closer to dying. Viewers of the film are invited to confront their mortality—come to terms with forms of dying and death as part of life—through the particular aesthetics and narrative framing of the filmmaker's role as mediators, in terms of crafting the film and also as people present with dying, crossing the abyss between audience and screen. This particular notion of space— often deemed as *sacred*, as in 'set apart'—illuminate Kairos as a kind of space where opportunities exist to *traverse* in ways that are non-sequential, without preconceived goals, and have the potential for learning toward new knowledge. In this way, Kairos is a space of opportunity, as in *krisis*. Further considerations in regard to 'traversing distances' and moving across spaces that set things apart, separateness, are discussed in Chapter 3, Movement and Thresholds.

Working with Situated Narratives

Situated Narratives is an exercise that relies on strategies of proximity and duration through the use of recorded images to charge discursive and non-discursive exchanges among multiple stakeholders. It is an approach for participatory synthesis and analysis within design research. The exercise is outlined and described through examples, following this chapter. When first designed, the workshop experience was called 'deconstructed scenarios,' as indeed the activities are aimed at expanding possibilities of sense-making through deep play with the structural elements of a scene, as drawn from video ethnography. The process is somewhat simple, while the preparation requires careful and thoughtful design by the research team. Stakeholders watch a short video of a nonfiction narrative scene, followed by an encounter with the deconstructed elements of the scene—key images presented as large photographs accompanied by a printed transcription of the dialogue—arranged on a table as a storyboard, as shown in Figure 2.3. The scene is exploded in space and suspended in time. The deconstruction might be likened to an architectural axonometric drawing—showing parts of a whole in relative location to one another yet separated. The deconstructed view, with materialized and movable narrative artifacts, affords an embodied experience for visualization—manipulations of what may or may not be seen. The still images and text extracted from the video provoke stakeholders to revisit moments from the moving-image narrative with greater thoughtfulness, care, and consideration. Collectively, the participants confront the image-oriented narrative elements and contribute questions, comments, and proposals through annotations and manipulations of the artifacts along with discussion. Lisbeth Frølunde describes "shifting, socially constructed understandings of texts" (the notion of text which includes a range of multimedia) through "facilitation and visual phenomena" as a neo-Bakhtinian dialogic approach, referencing Mikhail Bakhtin's theories of hybrid dialogic forms for efforts toward the generation of meaning (Frølunde 2014, p. 166; Bakhtin 1981). Situated Narratives, as an activity shared by multiple stakeholders, invites a diversity of perspectives and potentially surfaces 'ghost images and ideal types.' In this way, it is an activity of embodied learning for deconstructing documentary through discursive and nondiscursive exchanges.

I have conducted the exercise in-person as well as online. These experiences are different in that the materiality of printed matter and the bodily acts of moving physical objects in the company of other people is much more vibrant in terms of possibilities for discursive and nondiscursive exchanges. The engagement can produce insights when conducted online through the use of virtual video viewing and software mimicking interactive whiteboards, yet embodied learning through proximity is compromised.

At the same time, online applications of the exercise can offer the unique benefit of revisiting the deconstructed scene and participant contributions, affording iterations of analysis and further extending conversations for synthesis. The examples at the end of this chapter are drawn from in-person workshops held at Parsons School of Design.

Development of the exercise Situated Narratives was informed by Donna Haraway's perspectives on ways of seeing and ways of being that embrace "embodied objectivity that accommodates paradoxical and critical feminist science projects," as Haraway defines *situated knowledges* (Haraway 1988, p. 581). Proximity and duration are characteristics of narrative that support participatory research through what Haraway refers to as a persistence of vision and a call to "insist on the embodied nature of all vision and so reclaim the sensory system that has been used to signify a leap out of the marked body and into a conquering gaze from nowhere"—a gaze that claims objectivity by way of what Haraway refers to as the *god trick* (Haraway 1988, p. 581). It can be useful here to return to Marker and *Sans Soleil*, as this film in some ways illuminates Haraway's proposition that "Like 'poems,' which are sites of literary production where language too is an actor independent of intentions and authors, bodies as objects of knowledge are material-semiotic generative nodes" (Haraway 1988, p. 595). The image of Sarah Grossman, from the film *End of Life*, similarly performs in ways to counter and refute an objectifying gaze that might diminish complex personhood and make claims of objective truth about the process of dying.

The exercise Situated Narratives invites reckoning with moving and still images of the same scene through facilitated experiences to exploit dialectical possibilities. Perhaps the most notable historical example related to this kind of experience is the Zapruder film footage of the assassination of President John F. Kennedy in 1963. Abraham Zapruder, an amateur photographer, recorded the images of the assassination on Super-8 film, using a home movie camera (Sturken 1997). The Time-Life corporation purchased the footage from Zapruder for $150,000 and published still images from the Super-8 film in *Life* magazine one week after the event, while the film as moving images was restricted from public view for 12 years (Sturken 1997).

> The power of the film image lies precisely in its sequence of frames that appear to tell a story, a horrible story, with temporal precision. When *Life* publisher C.D. Jackson saw the film he reported to have been so disturbed that he had Time-Life acquire the motion-picture rights to it; although *Life* only needed print rights, Jackson wanted to suppress what the moving image showed. Certainly, the sequence is much more palatable as a succession of still images.
>
> (Sturken 1997, p. 28)

During the exercise Situated Narratives, participants move immediately from a setting of watching a scene as moving images to a table where the scene's elements, most dominantly still images extracted from the video, are printed as material artifacts and arranged as a storyboard. While the Zapruder example is charged with a national tragedy and the scrutinizing efforts of criminal investigation, the goals for Situated Narratives are open to expansive explorations and critique. It is important to consider the kinds of moving images that might charge the exercise. How might scenes be rendered and edited (or chosen from existing material) to provide fodder for speculation and debate in ways that raise issues of concern, ignite imaginations, and avoid didactic or preconceived opinions that might lead the witness? This is important and hard work for the design research team and indeed an imperfect process.

Ethnographic approaches have long contributed to transdisciplinary praxis, bridging conversations concerning participatory artistic- and design-based research with social science, affect, and media theories and practices. Ethnographic moving images can possess a range of varying aesthetic and affective qualities—they are not equal in these ways, just as a variety of visual strategies and narrative forms might constitute documentary. Ethnography has long been a practice utilized as a part of observational research, with a plethora of valuable and diverse approaches. This book does not attempt to endeavor discussions of ethnographic theories and methods comprehensively and rather focuses on certain aesthetic and conceptual aspects of images and narrative along with the analysis and synthesis of research artifacts, which may be ethnographic. The use of video ethnography in the exercise Situated Narratives presumes access to materials appropriate for the process. The example exercise at the end of this chapter shows details of all assets used for a particular workshop setting and ideally provides insights into what might be ideal characteristics for the video component. Sensory ethnography is an approach that I have employed in my practice and can often yield affective characteristics of proximity and duration, as argued in this discussion.

The film *Leviathan*, by Verena Paravel and Lucien Castaing-Taylor, is a work of sensory ethnography that utilizes proximity and duration for affecting visceral encounters and embodied learning (Castaing-Taylor, Paravel 2013). Filmed almost entirely with GoPro cameras—often strapped to the arms of fisherman or attached to long poles or ropes extended into the sea and sky from the fishing boat that the filmmakers used as an ethnographic site—*Leviathan* features images from the, sometimes dizzying, points-of-view of human and nonhuman participants. Fisherman, the boat's captain, live fish, dead fish, birds, the boat, nets, machinery, water, sky, wind, all serve as performative agents—subjects and objects—of sensorial encounters and counter-encounters. While the images are real and somewhat raw, they are also mediated through aesthetic manipulations—a visually poetic *ecriture*. The colors are vibrant, the black areas of the image provide deep contrasts, the movements are at times a magic-carpet ride, and the field-recorded audio has been enhanced to sonically produce new shapes within the space and time of the setting. The GoPro photography affords extra wide angles and radically close close-ups in motion. For some viewers, the film can be bombastic and destabilizing. Indeed, *Leviathan* invites, through proximity and duration, encounters with the harsh realities of commercial fishing—the killing and bloody handling of sea creatures, the impacts of hard labor on human bodies, and the precarity of the food chain and degradation of natural ecosystems resulting from systemic externalities of late capitalism. These images, for some viewers, provoke the kinds of confrontations that one might wish to *turn away from*. Encountering the film at cinematic scale—bright, bold close-up moving images projected on a large screen in a dark room—is far from an activity of passive consumption or escapist entertainment. *Leviathan* is an immersive experience that can be life affirming, spiritual, and profoundly provocative as a reminder of Gaia.

Sensory ethnography as an approach for participatory research can foster greater attunement with the richness and complexity of context within investigations. Video ethnography that privileges sensorial attunements must be carried out in ways that are sensitive to and accountable for the ethical considerations within relationships, especially in regard to images recorded within proximate and durational research experiences. Ernst Karel, an artist, researcher, key collaborator with Harvard's Sensory Ethnography Lab, as well as the sound designer for the film *Leviathan*, describes sensory ethnographic approaches in the online interview platform Ear Room,

> media anthropology or sensory ethnography is based on the understanding that human meaning does not emerge only from language; it engages with the ways in which our sensory experience is pre- or non-linguistic, and part of our bodily being in the world. It takes advantage of the fact that our cognitive awareness – conscious as well as unconscious – consists of multiple strands of signification, woven of shifting fragments of imagery, sensation, and malleable memory. Works of sensory media are capable of echoing or reflecting or embodying these kinds of multiple simultaneous strands of signification. Experiencing them constitutes an intellectual challenge for the viewer, who must actively bring their critical faculties to bear on the experience of the work, in effect to complete the work through their experience of it.
>
> (Wright 2013)

Our bodies are how we know that we exist. We sense spatio-temporal relationships through movement in coordination with information gleaned through the other senses. Yi-Fu Tuan states that, "movement is indeed life," while also taken for granted until we sense some lack in it, similar to our awareness of health (Tuan [1977] 1993, p. 36). The proximal senses of touch, taste, and smell are dependent on our ability to be close to things with our bodies. Sensing through sight and sound provides access to the world "out there," not so close to, or far away from, our physical beings (Tuan [1977] 1993, p. 35). Technology continuously evolves, for better or worse, our capacities for learning through redefined notions of proximity. Microscopes, telescopes, television, telephones, cameras, smartphones, airplanes, the Internet, and so on, all renegotiate notions of distance and 'out there.' Mediated narratives that provide forms of closeness can be both productive and destructive toward efforts of embodied learning. We can be close to things that are far away, while things close to us might remain remote to our awareness and understanding. Heidegger, in his essay "The Thing," challenges assumptions of proximity "What is happening here when, as a result of the abolition of great distances, everything is equally far and equally near? What is this uniformity in which everything is neither far nor near—is, as it were, without distance" (Heidegger [1971] 2001, p. 164)? Indeed, there are both benefits and liabilities brought about by technology that pointedly accelerates confusion in experiencing proximity. The notions of what might constitute modes of bodily presence are increasingly questionable as technologies accelerate. Two seemingly divergent paths might be observed as moving toward a future, where the physical body is no longer necessary, as the body image becomes supreme, or physical bodily presence gains hyper-elevated exchange value, and, at the same time, considering both paths in regard to emergent forms of the body as fetish and commodity within contexts of scarcity (Rinaldi, Carneiro Ribiero, Pollo 2017). These conditions raise deeply social concerns in terms of semio-capitalism—the escalating production of signs in a globalized and deterritorialized economy (Berardi 2009). There seem to be demands on our bodies to evolve within new relationships among labor, value, and time that are very precarious.

Proximity reverence

Reverence, or to revere—deep respect, to stand in awe of, from the Latin *revereri*, from *re-* (expressing intense force) + *vereri* 'to fear'—is a condition that can emerge from encounters taking place at proximate distances (revere 2010). Close encounters, as mimicked by the qualities of cinematic scale—the *plan rapproché* and *gros plan* of the close-up, often elicit reverence. The potential to revere might otherwise escape our senses where greater distances foster abstract recognition. Reverence can be a potent quality of embodied learning in terms of focusing parameters of respect and care for encounters. For example, we might imagine things we wish to say or do to our bosses, leaders, enemies, or romantic crushes, yet if they were to suddenly sit beside us our expressions would shift according to a certain *proximity reverence.*

Proximity challenges relationships with mortality. In preparation for our research with the *End of Life* project, I trained to become an end-of-life doula. The doula serves as a guide and collaborator to support the dying person to co-create what a good death might be for them. This role is an act of supporting and making manifest the visualizations of the dying person and navigating the best path toward these goals through whatever contingencies might arise. Perhaps the most striking characteristics of the doula practice are these acts of *collective visualization*—co-creating and ordering images, predicting what might be seen and planning how this might be manipulated through reflecting, listening and countering reflection. Time expands and contracts—there is not too little nor enough—in terms of how it is considered, discussed, navigated, and measured during the exchanges among doula, the dying person, and the surrounding caregivers and loved ones. In addition to learning how to provide services as a doula, the training also taught me about proximity and reverence in ways that one cannot easily imagine without the benefit of embodied learning.

While training as a doula, I encountered Timothy Pachirat's well-researched book, *Every Twelve Seconds: Industrialized Slaughter and the Politics of Sight*, which illuminates the complex notions of distance and proximity. Pachirat, a professor of political science, was employed for five and a half months as an entry-level worker at an Omaha industrial slaughterhouse without informing the management of his intentions to write about his experiences, on which the book centers. The first chapter opens with a provocative account of an event reported by the *Omaha World Herald* and featured on its front page. Six cattle on their way to slaughter escaped and ran through the Omaha town where two industrial slaughter facilities are located near one another. All of the animals were recaptured, except one that vehemently resisted and was shot and killed by police (Pachirat 2011).

The shooting took place during the ten-minute afternoon break for the workers at the second slaughterhouse. Venturing outside for fresh air, sunshine, and cigarettes, many of the slaughterhouse workers witnessed the killing of the animal firsthand, and during the lunch break the next day the news spread rapidly among the slaughterhouse employees, fueled by a graphic retelling by a quality-control worker who had been dispatched to the alleyway by slaughterhouse managers to observe the events and, later, to photograph the damage caused to the walls by the errant shotgun pellets. "They shot it, like, ten times," she said, her face livid with indignation, and her words sparked a heated lunch-table discussion about the injustice of the shooting and the ineptitude of the police. She began recounting the story of an unarmed man from Mexico who had recently been shot by the Omaha police. "They shot him just like they shot the cow," she asserted, to the nodding assent of her co-workers. "If he'd been white they wouldn't have shot him. You know, if you are Mexican in this country, the police will do anything to you."

(Pachirat 2011, p. 2)

These images are momentary flashes—exposures—of awkward realities that are otherwise disguised. Pachirat describes the slaughterhouse as "a place that is no-place," physically and socially hidden in plain sight, "an exemplary instance of how distance and concealment operate as mechanisms of power" (Pachirat 2011, p. 3). Collapsing distances and breaching systems of containment—whether these are physical barriers, secluded geographic locations, euphemisms, or laboring bodies performing the tasks that others wish to avoid—demand ways of seeing and being that are embodied and sensorial.

Images and narratives with qualities of proximal intensity can serve within visualization strategies in ways that shape and support environments of reciprocity and care.

Fredric Jameson has argued that "The visual is essentially pornographic, which is to say that it has its end in rapt, mindless fascination; thinking about its attributes becomes an adjunct to that, if it is unwilling to betray its object" (Jameson 1992, p. 1). While researching and making the film *End of Life*, I was continually asked, "why are you doing this?" Interest in a subject that no living creature avoids—mortality—was never an adequate answer. Friends and colleagues, many of whom are very smart and sophisticated, asked this question again and again, and often in a hushed whisper. Initially, I shared that my mother had recently died and that the circumstances of her death had raised interesting questions about hospice. Later, I answered the question by explaining that I had, many years before, spent several weeks editing a film in a hospital room with a close friend, the film editor James Lyons, who was dying and wished to be engaged in his craft up until the end of his life. But it wasn't until I was a few years into the making of the film *End of Life* that I came to understand from where my capacity for this particular curiosity had emerged: In 1985, I was a 21-year-old gay man living in New York City surrounded by people dying of AIDS and was told that I would most likely not survive. That experience—those images and narratives—transformed my perspectives, shaping my relationships with mortality through proximity and duration as integral to my ways of being in the world. Having this particular reckoning with my own mortality as certain within all its uncertainty, I came to understand dying as more than life at the very end. I was, and remain, intrigued and deeply curious around the wealth of knowledge that can be gleaned through experiences as we approach the end of life—to be close with dying—in ways that are generative, reciprocal, and caring. There can be great value in entropy, albeit a challenging space within which to coexist. To be present with dying as a part of being alive—to see the end of life as more than loss—informs and expands opportunities to learn, laugh, create, care, share, and transform with dying and with all stages of life and life's transitions.

In 1985, during my time as a student at the School of Visual Arts, the artist Hannah Wilke was one of my teachers. Between 1978 and 1982, Wilke had made a series of photographs of her mother who was suffering from cancer at the time. One piece of the series, titled *Portrait of the Artist with Her Mother, Selma Butter*, is a diptych: one image featuring Wilke, topless with randomly found objects decorating her breasts; the other image featuring her mother, also topless, revealing scars from a radical mastectomy. The diptych, while glaring in its comparative gestures, more than anything else evokes the trust and care of a close relationship over time. It is an image of grace, performing its presence and truth through the power of its situated persistence of vision. It denies both the portrayal of sympathetic victimhood and safe distance. Throughout the 1970s, Wilke employed her body as integral in her work across forms that included sculpture, performance, film, and photography. At the time, some feminists were critical of the way Wilke used her beauty to address issues of the male gaze. A calculated narcissism resonates from the flirtatious poses Wilke strikes in some art works. Her provocation was direct, as echoed in an early interview where Wilke asks, "Who has the guts to deal with cunts" (Schwartz 1972)? Wilke's performances of the feminine body/self are provocative counter-encounters. Her exaggerated poses—appearing immobilized as though already a picture—are strategies, "both to succumb to the 'gaze' (reiterating the normative tropes of femininity), and though such 'submission,' to immobilize it (like Medusa), forcing it to 'surrender'" (Jones 1998, p. 154). The images of Wilke's last collection of work, *INTRA-VENUS 1992–1993*, are poses of unrelenting presence—self-portrait photographs center her body as a site transformed through effects of cancer and treatments to combat the illness that would end her life in 1993 at age 52. The photographs are a kind of writing with fire, what Jill H. Casid refers to as *pyrographies*—enacting care through a rehearsal of death and negotiating ways to be present with the end of life (Casid 2012). Bald, bloated, and bandaged in some of the photos, Wilke performs to continue the conversation she had begun decades earlier, offering something to look at but not without spirited affect inviting reflection for the viewer (Smith 1994). Experiencing life in proximity to death—sensing through close-up images in non-sequential time—expands possibilities for embodied learning and knowing. Images and narratives with proximal and durational qualities have potential to provide greater affective resonance for meaning-making through expanding sensorial exchanges and reflections.

SITUATED NARRATIVES, WORKSHOP EXAMPLE

Situated Narratives is a design-based research exercise for engaging multiple stakeholders in discursive and nondiscursive critical exchanges through dynamic interactions with short videos (scenes) and their deconstructed visual and image-oriented elements. Situated Narratives can be used to support participatory synthesis and analysis, as well as co-creative efforts for proposing critical and speculative design scenarios.

Scenes used for the exercise might be an illumination of an 'image of crisis' (as described in Chapter 1, "Images of Crisis, Images of Change") and gathered during participatory fieldwork, as is the case for the examples provided here. The scenes might be defined as traditionally narrative—people or people-like characters within dynamic relationships to unfolding events, or beyond human-centric points of view. Ideally, a video scene is under ten minutes.

Outline of activities

I. Preparation for the workshop by the design team
  1. Refine key inquiry questions
  2. Select video scenes and draft short introductions for scenes
  3. Select key frames from videos and print these as photographs
  4. Transcribe dialogue of the scenes and print text in a large font size
  5. Make available other key references or artifacts (i.e. floor plans, objects)
  6. Assemble photos and printed dialogue as a storyboard on a table, covered in a writable surface (i.e. bond paper, markers), along with any other key artifacts
  7. Dedicate roles for the design team (facilitating, documenting)

8. Define, invite, and confirm participants, considering an inclusive stakeholder group

II. Activities
1. Share a brief introduction to the video scene
2. Participants watch the scene, ideally in a large format (projected or a big monitor)
3. Participants are invited to respond to the scene through engagement with the storyboard and artifacts, prompted by facilitators to annotate, highlight, move, or otherwise comment on the artifacts (inquiry questions might be introduced by facilitators)

This example is from an exercise that took place during the studio course Design for Living and Dying, as part of the Transdisciplinary Design MFA program at Parsons School of Design, The New School. The materials used in the exercise are research artifacts from the *End of Life* project, co-led by John A. Bruce and Paweł Wojtasik.

The details shared here are presented as reference examples only and do not represent a complete case study of activities and findings.

The workshop presented the exercise two times—each exercise used a different scene featuring the same main character, Carol Verostek. Carol was one of the five main characters from the feature-length film *End of Life*. The scenes used in the workshop were recorded during the research for the *End of Life* project but do not appear in the film. The scenes are identified as *Carol's Clinical Visit* and *Carol in Hospital.*

Participating stakeholders included a person with progressing terminal cancer, a patient with a slowly progressing terminal illness, a behavioral psychologist, a nurse practitioner, a member of the Patient Family Advocacy Council, an end-of-life doula, and the adult child of a recently deceased parent.

The framing for each scene, described below, was spoken aloud by one of the design team facilitators to the participating stakeholders before the videos were shown.

Carol's Clinical Visit

It is 2014. In 2003, 11 years ago, Carol was diagnosed with a rare form of terminal abdominal cancer. At that time, she was given six months to live. *The disease went into remission for five years, but then suddenly reappeared and nearly ended Carol's life. An experimental drug had been developed, and this worked to suspend the progression of cancer. Another five years passed, and Carol lived as she had previous to cancer—working, socializing, golfing, traveling, etc. Again, the cancer reemerged with near-fatal effects, and again another experimental drug was successful in reversing its course. In the spring of 2014, Carol, now 11 years after the initial diagnosis, expressed her status as, 'living with a time bomb inside of me.' She began, once more, to feel changes in her body and was tested to see if the cancer was progressing. In this scene, Carol visits her doctor to receive the test results. She knows that there are no other experimental drugs to try; hence, a reemergence would be very serious news.*

Carol in Hospital

Carol is in the hospital having suffered digestion challenges brought on by growing tumors from an aggressive cancer. This condition has prevented her from eating, and she must take in nutrients intravenously. She also suffers from pneumonia and is being treated with antibiotics. The scene takes place on a particular day when she is visited by a doctor and a social worker. She discusses her goals for leaving the hospital in order to go home and continue hospice care, as she understands her condition is beyond rescue treatment and her end of life is rapidly approaching. She also discusses plans for how she might make her home hospice environment most comfortable. Researcher/filmmaker John Bruce is present, along with Carol's sister Kathy, daughter Leslie, and husband Paul.

Participants engage with each scene as a discreet exercise. These scenes were chosen based on iterative discussions by the design research team and through posing and refining a set of key inquiry questions. For example: How might clinical settings and care-circle attunement capacities impact the information flows and decision-making capacities for patients experiencing serious illnesses? In what ways might critical care information be legible or illegible to patients and their care-circle within these settings? How might care-circle relationships exercise sensitivity in regard to the possible range of expectations that might emerge for patients?

Participants are guided to interact with the scene they have just watched as it is displayed in deconstructed form: key frames from the video printed as still images and transcribed dialogue printed as text

Figure 2.2 Situated Narratives workshop: participants watch the video scene *Carol's Clinical Visit* and engage with video artifacts as printed matter arranged on a table.

in large font, arranged along a table in the fashion of a storyboard. The printed materials are movable. Participants gather around the table with artifacts are invited to manipulate these artifacts—rearrange or cluster them, and also encouraged to write notes on the artifacts or the table, covered with paper, as shown in Figure 2.2. Markers and highlighters are made easily accessible for all. Interactions with artifacts from the scenes might include questions, highlights, lines, and arrows marking connections, and other forms to indicate comments.

Discursive exchanges among the participants were encouraged, while facilitation by the design team was limited to privilege open discourse. Facilitators occasionally asked questions to expand upon certain comments from participants or to prompt participants with high-level questions.

Findings and insights from the exercise example were rich, surprising at times, and informed subsequent lines of inquiry and research activities. The workshop was not intended to yield results to be published; therefore, I will share only a few anecdotal findings to further illuminate the exercise as an example.

During workshop activities responding to the video and artifacts from the video *Carol's Clinical Visit*, discussions and comments addressed issues concerning the use of technology, the seating arrangement, the appearance and language of the doctor, and a myriad of other productive observations. Most surprising was a deep conversation that emerged in response to a moment when Carol placed her hand on the doctor's knee in a gesture of camaraderie and compassion, as shown in Figure 2.3.

Figure 2.3 Situated Narratives workshop: artifacts from the video with comments and detail of Carol's gesture to the doctor.

The action transpired after Carol had noticed and inquired about a pin on the doctor's lapel. The doctor explained that the object was a gift from a patient who had recently died. Carol had just received the results of a test indicating that the terminal cancer she suffered from was not progressing at this time, and her outlook for the time being was encouraging. Carol's response to the doctor's loss of another patient, as signaled by the pin and made clear by his explanation, became a focus for the workshop participants—a rich 'image of crisis' spurring diverse perspectives and critiques regarding the pin, the doctor's explanation, and Carol's response. The dimensions of this discussion are too lengthy to fully describe here, while there were two opposing opinions worth noting. One participant, an end-of-life doula, remarked that Carol's expression of compassion for the doctor revealed a relationship of genuine reciprocity and care—Carol experienced the doctor as more than a service provider, and perhaps the doctor's expressions of care supported the conditions for this atmosphere of shared humanity. An opposing opinion, while agreeing that a caring relationship was evident and important, disagreed with the doctor's gesture of sharing that a patient had died. This participant's mother had recently died. They criticized the doctor for over-sharing in ways that might have been damaging to Carol's morale as a person with a terminal illness.

Findings generated through the exercise Situated Narratives are carefully collected and synthesized by the design team and, when appropriate, further synthesized collectively with the team and the participating stakeholders, through an ongoing, iterative, and generative process for gleaning insights to inform research and design.

This example shows the potential for the exercise Situated Narratives as a dynamic and productive environment for discursive and nondiscursive exchanges among multiple stakeholders.

***

References

Bakhtin, M.M. (1981) *The Dialogic Imagination: Four Essays*, ed. Michael Holquist, Austin: University of Texas Press.

Balsom, E. (2007) Saving the Image: Scale and Duration in Contemporary Art Cinema. *Cineaction*, October, Arts Premium Collection, p. 23.

Berardi, F. (2009) *Precarious Rhapsody: Semiocapitalism and the Pathologies of the Past-Alpha Generation*, London: Minor Compositions.

Berardi, F. (2015) *And: Phenomenology of the End*, Los Angeles: Semiotext(e).

Bergson, H. (2001) *Time and Free Will: An Essay on the Immediate Data of Consciousness*, Mineola, New York: Dover.

Bruce, J.A., Wojtasik, P. (Director) (2017) *End of Life*, New York, US: Grasshopper Films.

Casebier, A. (1988) A Deconstructive Documentary. *Journal of Film and Video*, Winter 1988, 40(1), pp. 34–39.

Casid, J.H. (2012) Pyrographies: Photography and the Good Death. *Women & Performance: A Journal of Feminist Theory* 22(1), pp. 109–131.

Castaing-Taylor, L., Paravel, V. (Director) (2013) *Leviathan*, New York, US: Cinema Guild.

Deleuze, G. [1985] (1989) *Cinema 2: The Time-Image*, Minneapolis: The University of Minneapolis Press.

Deleuze, G. (1991) *Bergsonism*, Brooklyn, New York: Zone.

Doane, M.A. (2021) *Bigger Than Life: The Close-up and Scale in the Cinema*, Kindle ed., Durham: Duke University Press.

Eames, C. (1977). *Powers of Ten and the Relative Size of Things in the Universe*, Eames Office. Retrieved August 9, 2016, from www.eamesoffice.com/the-work /powers-of-ten/.

Eisenstein, S. (1974) *Au dela les étoiles (Oeuvres, tome 1)*, Paris: U.G.E., p. 229; quoted in: Pascal Bonitzer, Here: The Notion of the Shot and the Subject of Cinema, trans. B. Krohn, *Film Reader 4*, eds. Blain Allen, Valentin Almendrarez, and WIlliam Lafferty, Evanston, Il., Northwestern University, 1979, p. 113.

Frølunde, L. (2014) Reflexive Learning through Visual Methods. In J. Simonsen, C. Svabo, S.M. Strandvad, K. Samson, M. Hertzum, O.E. Hansen, eds. *Situated Design Methods*, Cambridge, MA: MIT Press, pp. 161–180.

Guibert, H. (2014 [1982]) *Ghost Image*, trans. R. Bononno, Chicago: The University of Chicago Press.

Halberstam, J. (2011) *The Queer Art of Failure*, Durham: Duke University Press.

Haraway, D. (1988) Situated Knowledges: The Science Question in Feminism and the Privilege of Partial Perspective. *Feminist Studies* 14(3), pp. 575–599.

Heidegger, M. [1971] (2001) *Poetry, Language, Thought*, New York: Harper Perennial.

Jameson, F. (1992) *Signatures of the Visible*, New York, NY: Routledge, Chapman & Hall, Inc.

Jones, A. (1998) *Body Art/Performing the Subject*, Minneapolis, MN: University of Minnesota Press.

Latour, B. (2004) Why Has Critique Run out of Steam? From Matters of Fact to Matters of Concern. *Critical Inquiry* 30(2), pp. 225–248.

Marker, C. (Director) (1983) *San Soleil*, France: Argos Films.

Mirzoeff, N.D. (2011) The Clash of Visualizations: Climate Change and Counterinsurgency. *Social Research* 78(4), pp. 1185–1212.

Pachirat, T. (2011) *Every Twelve Seconds: Industrialized Slaughter and the Politics of Sight*, New Haven, CT: Yale University Press.

Petzold, C. (2018) (Director) *Transit*, Chicago: Music Box Films.

Reed, L. (1966) (Songwriter) "I'll Be Your Mirror". *Velvet Underground and Nico*, Verve.

revere (2010) *Oxford Dictionary of English*, 2nd ed., Oxford, England: Oxford University Press.

Rinaldi, D., Carneiro Ribiero, M.A., Pollo, V. (2017) Questões contemporâneas: Proximidade e imagem, entre a ética e o gozo, (Contemporary Questions: Proximity and Image, Between Ethics and Enjoyment). *Estudos e Pesquisas em Psicologia* 17(2), pp. 693–706.

Rosenbaum, J. (2007) Personal Effects: The Guarded Intimacy of Sans Soleil. *The Criterion Collection*, essays, June 25. Retrieved from https://www.criterion.com /current/posts/484-personal-effects-the-guarded-intimacy-of-sans-soleil.

Schwartz, B. (1972) Young New York Artists. *Craft Horizons (Archive: 1941–1978)* 32(5); ProQuest, p. 50.

Smith, R. (1994) An Artist's Chronicle of a Death Foretold. *The New York Times*, January 30.

Sturken, M. (1997) *Tangled Memories: The Vietnam War, the AIDS Epidemic, and the Politics of Remembering*, Berkeley, CA: University of California Press.

Suchman, Lucy (2002) Located Accountabilities in Technology Production. *Scandinavian Journal of Information Systems* 14(2), Article 7. Retrieved from http://aisel.aisnet.org/sjis/vol14/iss2/7.

Tuan, Y. [1977] (1993) *Space and Place: The Perspective of Experience*, Minneapolis: The University of Minneapolis Press.

Wright, M.P. (2013) Interview with Ernst Karel, *EAR ROOM*, February 14, Retrieved from https://earroom.wordpress.com/2013/02/14/ernst-karel/.

3   Movement and thresholds

Transitions are thoughts and actions that move across thresholds—movements from one state of being and knowing to another. Movement is life. "In movement we hunt and are hunted; return home and become strangers; communicate with our parents when still in the womb; relax, work, trade in the market, and generate images of each other in fleeting encounters" (Mollona 2021, p. 4). The ease, or lack thereof, of movement calls into question the forces that accelerate or impede the capacity to engage in transitions, to cross thresholds. Boundaries function to separate and enclose—to inhibit movements. Borders, barriers, or gaps might be material or manifest in forms of perception that direct and shape relationships according to proximity and duration. Boundaries might be spaces—the distances between here and there. These spaces and dividing lines define positions and contextualize identifying criteria—things that are *in* versus things that are *out*, close or far away, 'with us or against us,' and so on.

Borders can be a big problem. Philosophically and practically, borders have largely evolved to exert power and control. There is an abundance of historical accounts, allegories, rationales, and other examples and narratives that valorize and critique borders—from the Great Wall of China and levees for coastal flood protection to the chain-link fences of suburban backyards. Nation-states enact what are perhaps the most legible and fortified borders by way of systems of checkpoints and passport controls, evidenced through several vivid historical and contemporary examples. The 19th-century lazarettos—specially designed structures for housing the quarantine of passengers, animals, personal possessions, and merchandize—of the then-thriving port on the island of Syros operated according to the 1845 Sanitary Code in Greece, categorizing danger according to places of origin (Kondylatou 2020). "Fundamental was the distinction of places between sanitary immune and non-sanitary immune, which in their turn were divided into clean, suspect, and unclean" (Kondylatou 2020, p. 50). The 'health' of a nation, in political terms, is maintained through order and the 'right' balance of

DOI: 10.4324/9780367365264-3

hierarchies (Kondylatou 2020). The image of society has form–contours shaped by characteristics of identity–a profile described by Mary Douglas as being one where, "its outlines contain the power to reward conformity and repulse attacks" (Dounglas [1966] (1980), cited in Kondylatou 2020, p. 22). The lazarettos were described, according to journal accounts from that time, as being like prisons—guarded, shabby, without proper protection from the elements, and generally very harsh. Class was a factor in the degree of comfort during lazaretto quarantine, as wealthy passengers could pay for better food and more luxurious amenities (Kondylatou 2020). Barriers that are more insidious, such as those used to instigate and enforce social and economic stratification, might be argued as some of the most dangerous and deadly forms of borders. The process for applying to an institution of higher education, filing tax returns, gaining access to healthcare, voting, and navigating participation within policy-making and governance are a few examples of where border design violence might emerge. Too often, it seems, the spaces just beyond the edges of people, places, and things have become sites for treacherous devices of abusive agents.

Borders can also be edges and buffer zones—*spaces in between*—where open investigations and exchanges take place. For example, our research with the *End of Life* project explores experiences at the end of life through collapsing distances that separate perspectives of living from dying, engaging with notions of sacred space—places of reverence and awe. The word 'sacred,' from Latin *sacrare*, from *sacer, sacre-* 'holy' means to be connected with God or a god, or dedicated to a religious purpose and so deserving veneration (sacred 2010). Mary Douglas discusses *sacer* as also meaning restriction, as the term Holy is based on the idea of separation, sometimes translated from the Hebrew root k-d-sh as 'set apart' (Douglas [1966] 1984, p. 8). The idea of separateness permeates historical notions for the possibilities of approaching sacred space—moving toward mystery and transcendence. Transdisciplinary approaches—moving across and beyond—can serve as pedagogies for facilitating transitions through buffer zones. Co-creative learning through making in these kinds of generative spaces can serve sense-making and decision-making to inform transformations for a more just, equitable, and sustainable future. This chapter considers the ways participatory design, through the use of images and narratives, can facilitate activities of collective identification as these relate to movements across thresholds, at individual and system scales.

Lost in space, or how I stopped worrying and learned to love between-ness

Becoming is an act of organization that begins with identity formation—whether this occurs for a single-cell organism, a person, a group, an institution, a nation-state, or at other scales of belonging. The formation of identity emerges through behaviors that engage decision-making for determining that which exists inside the boundary for containing the attributes of identity versus things outside of the boundary. These determinations are nodal positions, criteria, qualities, beliefs, and other identifying elements of a system that are in motion—in flux and in relationships, constantly configuring and reconfiguring as a constellation that is *becoming*. The politics of identity are contingent on behavior and thus raise questions: In what ways might the threshold—a border, membrane, or space in-between—be permeable, navigable, or negotiated, and how might these characteristics affect multidirectional movements of *becoming* and *unbecoming*? In order to introduce this notion of identification and identity formation when teaching, I will often sketch, very quickly, a simple diagram—first, drawing a sloppy circle, adding nodes (crosses and naughts) inside of and outside of the circle, then erasing parts of the circle, and, lastly, drawing arrows that traverse the permeable boundary. The content details of the crosses and naughts are the stuff that's *least important*, I would emphasize while making the sketch. What matters most are the spaces and ways for movement. While an undergraduate student, I once witnessed a teacher of Hindu philosophy attempt to illuminate the idea of sharing and gaining knowledge as proposed in the stories of the Bhagavad Gita. She drew a wine glass on the blackboard and then ran around the room, waving her arms in the air and exclaiming that wine was not in the glass but was instead everywhere. This was an idea I could get with. Certainly, there are many philosophical examples for contemplating movement across thresholds, perspectives for acts of identification, and ways for learning and acquiring new knowledge. The Japanese philosophy of *Ma* offers a valuable perspective on the learning possibilities of between-ness.

Yoko Akama, in her article, "Being awake to *Ma*: designing in betweenness as a way of becoming with," describes *Ma*, in relation to design, as a way for awakening our senses—developing sensibilities for the unknown, invisible, or energetic potential of emptiness (Akama 2015). *Ma* is translated in the English language as 'space.' The concept of *Ma* is used in several contexts, from architectural notions of physical space to spiritual practices concerning meditative space. The essence of what might be called an 'invitation for opportunity' arises through considerations of the in-between-ness of space. Between-ness speaks to relational qualities and the possibilities for co-designing to facilitate transitional movements. In this way, *Ma* resonates with participatory design practices focused on addressing complex social and environmental challenges—the ways design might embrace "creating, transforming, and *becoming together* among heterogeneity—among beings and non-beings, systems and power, and among places and atmospheres—by immersion in *emergence* and *chance*" (Akama 2015, p. 262, original emphasis). Akama links the notion of space, according to *Ma*, with what Bruno Latour refers to as 'plasma'—everything that remains unconnected—"that which is not yet formatted, not yet mastered, not yet socialized, not yet engaged in metrological chains, and not yet covered, surveyed, mobilized, or subjectified" (Latour 2005, p. 254, as cited in Akama 2015, p. 264). *Ma* can be space that grounds co-creative activities to yield what Akama calls 'fragments'—anecdotal moments, reflections, points of convergence—and in turn generate resonant meanings that are hard to measure (Akama 2015). *Ma* "requires a shift in consciousness from being *subject*-centered to *absence*-centered"—inviting greater attention to the hints, contours, or traces that conjure expansive understandings and imaginings (Akama 2015, p. 265). Many of the ideas related to *Ma* have been part of the discussion throughout this book, especially in regard to explorations of proximity and duration, as well as through examples shared from the film *End of Life*. Coincidently, when I shared *End of Life* with a long-time friend, John Oglevee, his immediate response was to reference *Ma*. Oglevee is a Noh scholar and Director of Theater Nohgaku in Tokyo. Noh is a form of Japanese drama, performed with masks and songs, having evolved from Shinto rites. He wrote to me:

> Noh is based on *Ma*. We spend a lot of time working on the *Ma*. While there is the somewhat cliched trope about Jazz being about what is not played, there are usually so many notes in Jazz that the absence is less evident. In Noh, and what I see in my first viewing of your film, it is indeed the *Ma* that creates the mass in this. So much of the scholarship in my field has focused on the stories left behind and so many films of "the aged" or "dying" tell their stories. Your film has captured humanity. I believe that this is also what is at the core of Noh. It's ringing a bell and letting the resonance fill in the rest. The ripples in the pond.

Ma might be imagined as a conductive atmosphere for resonance—movements of energetic vibrations through space and time and aligned with notions of reverberation. Reverb, in acoustics, is sound waves emanating and moving through the environment of the original source of the sound, continuing after this source has stopped production. Vibrations. For instance, an incident might incite a protest or riot—a crowd forms and is motivated to behave in certain ways, and later disperses. Zeitgeists, trends, and other forms of cultural conversations are legible through reverberations—traces of behavior, while attempts to understand their essence is achieved by reading between the lines, in the *Ma*. Narrative forms that embrace notions of *Ma* through aesthetic and performed approaches can be ways to make legible the reverberations within complex systems. Narrative can illuminate the richness of dynamic relationships—support reading between the lines— that are the reverberations within constellations of *becoming*, of movements toward thresholds of transition and transformation.

Interdependence offers another perspective on *Ma*. The concept of inter- dependence is sometimes visualized as a web of connections—nodes joined by lines. Attention is often focused on the nodes—the things, elements, people, places—rather than the lines of connection. Connections are not simply agnostic glue or predetermined coded highways for relationships to travel upon. The lines illustrating 'connections' within interdependence are reverberating, conjunctive, and symbiotic activities of the exchange. The mass of the 'plasma' or churn of interdependence might be a myriad of real or abstract dynamic activities—dancing, battling, playing, confront- ing, exchanging, and other opportunities for actively embracing emergence. Symbiosis is a model for understanding conjunctive exchange. The scientist Lynn Margulis dedicated much of her life's work to examine the central role of symbiosis in the creation of new life forms. Symbiosis is the process of bringing together unlike entities to create new complex entities, merging and continuing this process to form larger multiunit symbiotic individuals capable of greater inclusive integration of other entities, and so on (Margulis 1998). We live in a symbiotic world. Our human bodies came to be from a long series of coexisting relationships and mergers. Darwinian theories of selection for understanding how species adapt and change are not the entire story regarding the ways organisms evolve. Collective learning and ways of knowing are processes of symbiosis—intricate partnerships, co-creative expressions, contingencies, and interdependence—the effervescent stuff of *becoming*.

Design dramaturgy

The power of cinema is often said to be experienced as *moving*. The notion of being moved by the movies—by moving image narratives— might simply be understood as the stirring of emotions, while the move- ment of one's perspectives and opinions can be a transgressive activity. Cinematic narrative can invite ways to grapple with and identify rela- tionships within complex situations. What's going on here, what is this, why are things transpiring in certain directions, where do I position myself in relation to these people, things, and activities? These ques- tions, and others, are central to the deep play that serves to help viewers discern and relate to the stakes and dimensions of narrative situations. In this way, cinema is a form of systems thinking—manipulating variables among causal relationships.

Dramaturgy is *seeing in systems*—engaging in visualization—suspecting what can be seen and manipulating it. Dramaturgy, in theater and cinema, is the process of organizing narrative elements to produce a particular journey and outcome of the story experience. The elements of a drama are the variable nodes of a dynamic interactive system. Variables can be manipulated to create images that propose ideas, beliefs, stakes, mystery, jeopardy, and a host of other dramatic elements. The composition of particular variables creates the dynamics of a scene. Shaping and working with 'images of crisis' and 'images of change,' as discussed in Chapter 1, is dramaturgy. Scenes, as variables of narrative drama, are leverage points—places to intervene in a system. Intervening in systems through the identification of leverage points are acts of designing conditions for atmospheres that support the emergence of desired outcomes—strategies for transformative change.

Dramaturgy can be carried out in a variety of process formats. Models for dramaturgy as a collective practice might be found in theater companies with shared leadership, or in the 'writers room' of a television series—collaborative spaces for co-creating *storyworlds* to guide narrative development and for co-designing mise-en-scène to inform material expressions. The process of moving-making, while collaborative, less often assumes a flat hierarchy for setting dramaturgical intentions, as these decisions reside primarily with writers and directors. A myriad of reasons might contribute to hierarchies within cinema production—market-driven controls of authorship and ownership and the mythologies of the auteur are perhaps dominant factors. Nevertheless, I propose that a more democratized process for the creation and circulation of dramaturgy experiments, especially as cinematic forms, can serve as a potent approach for exploring identification and progressive movements toward greater equity and justice. The perspectives of researchers and designers are often too limited in regard to the possibilities for using moving image narratives as part of their practice. Certainly, there is great utility in video recording and video ethnography as a way to document field observations and interviews, or to create references of other research and design processes. However, the use of moving images and narratives offers a much wider range of dynamic possibilities within participatory design learning environments. Cinematic tropes can serve as a unique set of devices for co-creating visualizations. These expressions can be used to manipulate possible ways of seeing and provide stakeholders with experiences for rich exchanges that support embodied and collective learning. Cinematic dramaturgy uses image-oriented artifacts for manipulating leverage points of a system—working with the *Ma*—the between-ness of narrative and audiences.

The film *Charlie Pisuk* is an example of the ways cinematic dramaturgy can inform provocative prototypes—provotypes—that support participatory design research processes.

The short film, created and performed by a media collective of Indigenous people, explores issues concerning communication and identification. *Charlie Pisuk* opens with images of a village, including a super-imposed caption reading "Igloolik, Nunavut, Canada," followed by intertitles over black:

> The Barratt Impulsiveness Scale is the most widely used self-report measure of impulsive personality traits. Initially developed in the United States of America, the B.I.S. has been applied around the world. Several family members of "subject #112" known for his instable behavior agreed to participate in the following case study. Names of participants withheld.
>
> (Arnait Video Productions 2015)

Over the course of the nearly 18-minute duration of the film, a series of interviews is conducted, administering the Barratt Impulsiveness Scale (BIS). The camera's frame for all interviews is the same—a medium-wide shot, head-and-shoulders, of a person sitting in what looks to be a very modest kitchen. Each interview subject is identified by a caption indicating their relationship to Subject #112. The BIS is administered by an off-screen voice, possessing a generically authoritative tone. The BIS proceeds through posing statements in regard to the person in question—in this case Subject #112 and asks the family members to respond with 'rarely,' 'sometimes,' 'often,' 'always,' or 'don't know.' Excerpts from two of the interviews in *Charlie Pisuk* reveal the complex dynamics of these exchanges:

BIS administrator: He plans his tasks carefully.
Step-cousin of Subject #112: Sometimes. But I don't know if he plans carefully.
BIS administrator: He is carefree.
Step-cousin of Subject #112: Yes, he cares about everybody.
BIS administrator: Often or always?
Step-cousin of Subject #112: Always. But sometimes he doesn't care.
BIS administrator: So, sometimes?
Step-cousin of Subject #112: Yeah (nods). When he's caring, he cares a lot.
BIS administrator: He has a tendency to walk and move fast.
Step-cousin of Subject #112: Sometimes. Yeah. When you walk slow, he can walk slow, too. So, I don't know if he walks fast or you walk fast. So, when you walk slow, he can walk slow, too. Often. But sometimes he walks fast. Yeah.
BIS administrator: He finds it hard to sit still for long periods of time.

Niece of Subject #112: He has lots of kids, I've heard. He has lots of kids. I don't know if there are 3 or 4, but maybe 5. I can't believe I don't know how many kids he has. He is my uncle. Always.

BIS administrator: He has a tendency to change housing.

Niece of Subject #112: Housing? I don't think … he doesn't live in the house, I mean, he does live in the house but I think he made that house … I heard he owns the house, but I think he has a tendency to change house if he wants to move to a housing house. Housing house?

BIS administrator: He makes plans ahead of time.

Niece of Subject #112: I've seen him pack in less than 15 minutes. So, I would say, rarely, no not rarely. Sometimes? Yeah, sometimes or often. Yeah, often.

(Arnait Video Productions 2015).

The BIS is met with a range of responses that counter the inquisition and offer speculative wisdom. These uncanny forms of counter-encounters are performed by Indigenous people who are non-actors playing fictional versions of themselves. The off-screen, almost robotic voice that administers the BIS is juxtaposed with the richness of the 'family members.' The responses delivered by family members chip away at the rigidity and flattening qualities of the inquiry to expose its inappropriateness, and, at the same time, satirically punch holes in the notion of 'documentary.'

Charlie Pisuk is a stylized cinematic rendering of a re-enactment. Working as part of the collective Arnait Video Productions, each performer in *Charlie Pisuk* created their role and contributed to the film's overall concept. Arnait is part of the coalition Isuma.TV—a collaborative multimedia platform for Indigenous filmmakers and media organizations (Isuma.TV 2021). While the BIS is an actual survey (in use today) and has perhaps contributed to the violent systems of oppression imposed by the Canadian government on Indigenous people, the narrative is a calculated farce designed as critique. The film is a process exercise and an approach to learning through making, similar to the 'image of crisis' and 'image of change' videos produced by the Hum design research team, as shared in Chapter 1. Additionally, *Charlie Pisuk* functions as a completed film to intentionally engage audiences in an embodied learning experience. It is a hybrid film—comprising elements of fiction and nonfiction, the effects of which can be unnerving for some viewers. The film's cringe-worthy car-crash of miscommunication is in turn funny, confusing, and a searing condemnation of the efficacy of the BIS (if reading the film carefully). *Charlie Pisuk's* impact is more than a clever twist in that the conceit of the film portrays oppressive dynamics that are not merely abstractions for the performers, for they have likely been subjected to very similar and very real, demoralizing, colonial, and destructive exchanges. Marie-Hélène Cousineau, a co-founder of Arnait who lived in the Nunavut community for many years and was a collaborator in creating *Charlie Pisuk*, posted this comment about the film on the IsumaTV website:

It is funny that people do not realize that the actors were actually making fun of situations in which they find themselves sometimes … Yes it is a real questionnary [sic] that is used by scientists and the film wants to show that it is not culturally appropriate! The actors came up with characters and improvised … We had a week to create the characters, and learn improvisations. They came up with costumes and attitudes …. I hope now it is clearer … It is a comedy not a real documentary.

(IsumaTV 2021)

In some ways, *Charlie Pisuk* is an example of the 'performance of ethnography,' an approach developed by the anthropologists and educators Victor and Edith Turner (Turner, Turner 1982). To perform ethnography is to embody a performance role in fulsome ways—to move and be moved within it—allowing relational dynamics to unfold and incorporating reflective practices in ways that blur subjective and objective perspectives. The videos by the Hum design team, as shared in Chapter 1, are also an example of performing ethnography. The performance of ethnography relies on the creative control of information—the way a performer frames expressions for audiences. People, as agents within systems of service, perform their roles as considered through frames of representation. Examining performance frames is also used in *service design* approaches for understanding the different perspectives of stakeholder engagements, for example, 'front of house' activities versus 'back of house' activities. Think of a restaurant's kitchen staff as they exchange information with one another through discursive and nondiscursive exchanges, as compared to their interactions with wait staff as they pick up dishes from the kitchen and, in turn, as wait staff deliver dishes to the dining clientele. The framing of performance becomes even more complex in contexts for health care, social, and other civic services. These considerations are key concepts and practices of service design (Penin 2018). The theory of framing, as introduced by Gregory Bateson and expanded upon by many other social scientists including Erving Goffman, involves dramaturgy and visualization.

To frame is to discriminate a sector of sociocultural action from the general on-going process of community's life. It is often reflexive, in that, to "frame," a group must cut out a piece of itself for inspection (and retrospection). To do this it must create – by rules of exclusion and inclusion – a bordered space and a privileged time within which images and symbols of what has been sectioned off can be "relived," scrutinized, assessed, revalued, and, if need be, remodeled and rearranged.

(Turner, Turner 1982, p. 34)

Non-actors playing themselves within experiments utilizing the performance of ethnography require self-reflection and imagination. This is especially true for unscripted or semi-scripted scenarios. Improvisation can be a challenging form of expression, despite this kind of performance being thought of as somewhat 'natural' or relative to one's reality. Inhabiting a role through improvisational strategies demands shifting between self-conscious and intuitive behaviors. Play-acting through mockery and satirical representations is no less rigorous, as devices for humor rely on multi-layered and nuanced references. Samuel R. Delaney's *Dhalgren* is a novel that takes place in a near future and is set in a city recovering from an undisclosed calamity. The main character, named Kid, reflects on performance:

Actions are interesting to watch. [Kid thinks.] I learn about the actors. Their movements are emblems of the tensions in this internal landscape, which their actions resolve. About to act is an interesting state to experience, because I am conscious of just those tensions. Acting itself feels fairly dull; it not only resolves, it obliterates those tensions from my consciousness.

(Delaney [1975] 1996, p. 440)

The quote from *Dhalgren* underlines a critical point that is central to the performance of ethnography and embodied learning. The moment of being 'about to act'—poised, in a state of imminence and anticipation—elevates the consciousness and reflection of internal tensions that can be exciting—thrilling even, and also at times deeply uncomfortable. Anticipation and expectation are nouns that are often used interchangeably, while they are different. Both are acts of looking forward to something happening. Anticipation can be thought of as an act associated with *futuring*—a way of being that is actively and excitedly open to possibilities that might occur, even those we cannot imagine. Expectation is an act of looking forward to things happening with an attitude of entitlement or a preconceived notion of what is to come.

The notion of tensions producing 'emblems' in an internal landscape resonates with the ideas of 'images of crisis' and 'images of change' as discussed in Chapter 1. Emblems of our reflections are the recollection-images, as discussed in Chapter 2, that we conjure in anticipation, within the supreme opportunity of *krisis*—a moment demanding a decision. Movement resolves tensions—crosses a threshold beyond anticipation.

Anticipation can impact our capacities of perception. The video of Ram Dass, as described in detail in Chapter 1, anonymously and silently staring back at the viewer for a duration of nearly seven minutes and seemingly about to speak, provokes tremendous anticipation. The space between the viewer and Ram Dass—the *Ma*—extends beyond the amount of time typically expected to elapse before receiving some kind of action or new information from a cinematic experience. The initial, entitled expectation is for the man to speak. When this does not occur, sense-making might respond to expectations through the conclusion that he is unable to speak, and perhaps because of his age this is a medical condition. The extended space and time afford more opportunities, and expectation ideally gives way to anticipation, opening new possibilities for identification. If not a medical condition, then what? Is the man a trickster? Are there other things to pay closer attention to—the sounds of footsteps, chimes, a passing airplane heard off-screen? Are the movements of the man's eyes signaling that he holds a secret, perhaps the source of his silence, perhaps he's been told by the filmmakers to refrain from speaking? Is his silence an identifying feature of his victimhood or a device of his power to command attention and set the terms for the unspoken conversation between the image and the viewer? Anticipation might be considered as the energetic spaces that reside among states of being (or the between-ness), described through notions of potentiality, actuality, and impotentiality. Giorgio Agamben devotes extensive thought and discussion to the Aristotelian notions of potentiality, describing its essence:

> To be potential means: to be one's own lack, *to be in relation to one's own incapacity*. Beings that exist in the mode of potentiality *are capable of their own impotentiality*, and only in this way do they become potential. They *can be* because they are in relation to their own non-Being. In potentiality, sensation is in relation to anesthesia, knowledge to ignorance, vision to darkness.
>
> (Agamben 1999, p. 182)

Attempting to make sense of illusions, like sleight-of-hand magic tricks, provides another way to consider anticipation in relation to potentiality and impotentiality. Merlin Sheldrake shares an anecdote in his book, *Entangled Life: How Fungi Make Our Worlds, Change Our Minds, and Shape Our Futures*, about a magician who performs at a restaurant (Sheldrake 2020). Returning restaurant guests often shared with the magician their stories about unusual sensorial experiences that occurred after having encountered the illusions of his magic act. One guest reported that the color of the sky was more brilliant, wondering if his drink had been spiked. Others reported being more fascinated with seeing patterns and being more attentive to the refreshing qualities of rain. The magician's explanation for these reports is the disruption of expectation. Sheldrake explains that the effects of witnessing the magic acts opened new pathways for sense-making—other possible ways of sensing that have been there all along. A magic trick misdirects attention and creates a blind spot by removing evidence that would ordinarily support causal logics, suspending the economy of our brain's sense-making network activities. Ordinarily, without being conscious our minds fill in the blanks, we leap to *knowing*. Through encounters with magic, instead of getting what we expect something else emerges. This suspension of tendencies of expectation can linger and thus force our senses to engage more fully (Sheldrake 2020). Mycelium, the vegetative part of fungi, is a network that performs digestive and communicative activities. Psilocybin mushrooms (magic mushrooms), one of the many kinds of fruiting bodies of mycelium, are affective in similar ways—rerouting expectations and opening up the potential of sensorial experiences. Certainly, many kinds of biochemical experiences can produce shifts in perception, for example, activities that increase the levels of endorphins or dopamine and a myriad of other conditions that prompt similar neuropsychological changes. Opening spaces for greater sensorial perceptions and expanding the agency of anticipation can be potent conditions for supporting collective understandings and effervescence.

Opening *spaces* for learning, working with the *Ma*, points to questions for how participatory design processes might embody forms of pedagogy that create conditions for *movement* toward thresholds of transformation. Raul Zibechi, in his book *Territories of Resistance: A Cartography of Latin American Social Movements*, proposes that social movements flourish where education is an *education in movement*, embracing transgressive notions of pedagogy that center the basis of learning on the climate of human relationships (Zibechi 2012). Pedagogy that embodies and models collective movement toward transformation often exists in conflict with intuitional forms and processes. Individualism is at the heart of these troubles. Disciplinary rigidity, or impermeability, can also be a barrier. Institutions, including those of higher education, are rife with systems of recognition and reward that deeply privilege individual authorship, ownership, and vertical hierarchies. The notion of the commons as a space for a pedagogy of movement—"enclosures that remain open"—can provide opportunistic learning environments that churn with productive combustion, conflicted within or alongside intuitional realms, while pushing back against disciplinary limits and neoliberal value systems (Mollona 2021). Modeling a pedagogy of movement within learning collectives is integral for embodying participatory artistic- and design-based research. Parallel education and social movements have a rich history and ongoing trend of convergence that produces fertile forms of the commons within these notions of pedagogy of movement. Massimiliano Mollona, in his book, *Art/ Commons: Anthropology beyond Capitalism*, discusses the profile and work of the Institute of Radical Imagination (IRI). IRI is described as "a group of curators, activists, scholars and cultural producers with a shared interest in co-producing research, knowledge, artistic and political research-interventions, aimed at implementing post-capitalist forms of life" (Institute of Radical Imagination 2021). An extensive history of initiatives and thought leaders have contributed to the lineage of learning and social transformation in ways aligned with notions of education in movement, from Mary McLeod Bethune, Helen Keller, and Ivan Illich to Paulo Freire, Community Indigenous Schools, Ericka Huggins and the Oakland Community School, Fred Moten, Stefano Harney, and Ruth Wilson Gilmore, to name only a few. Transdisciplinary approaches are integral to educating in movement. In my roles as both an educator and a transdisciplinary researcher, I am vigilant in bringing my students, colleagues, and the communities I participate within outside the boundaries of their institutions and workplaces.

Getting real and uncomfortable, identification and identity

Transdisciplinary approaches are affective ways for *breaking the fourth wall*—the imaginary boundary not only separating performers from audiences but also separating the places for accessing and exchanging ideas, perspectives, frames of reference, situated knowledges, and other new ways of learning and knowing. Transdisciplinary modes for learning through narrative and performance benefit through a myriad of experiments and forms that leverage aspects of the performance of ethnography, hybrid (non) fiction, re-enactment, and other gestures that break the fourth wall. The Theater of the Oppressed and its branches, books and films of historical fiction, camp and drag, and many other performance formats can be useful models worthy of examination for approaches to embodied learning within participatory research processes. However, the volume of rich examples is too vast to address in the scope of this discussion. Further, it is perhaps important to note that participatory design practices need not master theater arts or cinema production in order to leverage approaches that use performance and frames. Basic skills are all that is required for working with images and narratives, as discussed throughout this book, for supporting efforts of collective learning and movement.

Framing, as a way for creatively manipulating information for audiences, is rendered cinematically through performance as well as through the aesthetics of images, mise-en-scène, and montage—fragments, anecdotes, and sketches—that serve as useful traces in the *plasma*, in the *Ma*. Matthew

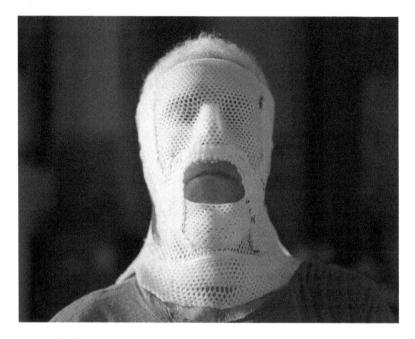

Figure 3.1 Matthew Freedman performing with a radiation mask, production photo during filming *End of Life*, 2017.

Freedman performs in the film *End of Life* through frames that position him as an artist and as a person experiencing terminal illness. In one scene, he wears a mask that he had previously worn as part of his radiation treatments for cancer, as shown in Figure 3.1. Matt's re-enactment utilizes costume and storytelling to vividly and poetically perform his experiences: "I would be shot with these proton beams from three different angles. I had tumors in my neck they would attack this way, and a salivary gland under my tongue they would get at this way" (Bruce, Wojtasik 2017). Later, in the same scene, Matt switches from the first person to the second person: "The strange thing about going through this is you can hear the machinery of the accelerator that's directing the beams at you, clicking and banging" (Bruce, Wojtasik 2017). Matt, in his role as a performance artist, uses his skills to draw the audience into the image he creates. The re-enactment leverages poetic license and takes on mysterious and provocative qualities. Cinematic affordances accentuate the performance through rendering Matt's speech as voiceover and freeing the image for greater stylization—his tongue stretches in odd ways, pokes out of his mouth and through a hole in the mask, and imitates the exercises he performed during his recovery after the treatments. The combination of the mask and the motions of his tongue complicate notions of struggle with gestures of comedy. The scene displays an embodied reflection and invites the viewer to confront the experience of radiation through a subjective account. The image is rendered as a medium shot with Matt composed dead-center in the frame and surrounded by a dark abyss. Considering the laws of cinematic scale, the image is balanced in its proximate intensity—not too close or too far—avoiding the grotesque while maintaining a desired tension through awkwardness.

Carol Verostek appears in the film *End of Life* as healthy and radiant. She reflects on her proximity to dying, reciting poetry during medical treatments. In another scene, Carol agrees to perform her ritual of applying cosmetics, as shown in Figure 3.2.

Carol: This is called "Boost." If you have puny eyebrows, it gives you a little extra umph. Theoretically, I have something that resembles what used to be eyelashes. Why do I do this? I don't know. Part vanity, part self-help and motivation.

(Bruce, Wojtasik 2017)

Carol performs self-reflection, literally making a comment about her continued vanity as it collides with her mortality. The steps of her beauty regime

Figure 3.2 Carol Verostek performing her cosmetic ritual in the film *End of Life*, 2017.

are completed very quickly at the beginning of the scene, and I am heard, off-screen while operating one camera (Wojtasik, the other camera), asking Carol to repeat the actions. Carol responds to the request with a smirk that feigns annoyance, while her actions comply with the direction. Carol says, "I'm going to kill you, both. You happy now" (Bruce, Wojtasik 2017)? In this way, Carol makes known her role as a participating director of the film's scene. She is not an object of focus for documentary cameras. Her status as dying, while beyond her control, does not serve as the dominant representation of her personhood. The performances of Carol Verostek and Matt Freedman in the film *End of Life* engage in a kind of 'frame slippage,' as understood according to Goffman, shifting their relationships with and within the narrative in ways that provoke the attention of the film audience, ideally spurring self-reflection and embodied learning for viewers, by proxy (Goffman 1986).

In the short film, *This Lemon Tastes of Apple*, the film's director, Kurdistan-Iraq born artist Hiwa K, and collaborators, situate themselves in the action of an actual street protest in progress. The subgroup, if it is indeed one, enacts a performance comprising spoken word accompanied by guitar and harmonica. They are otherwise fully integrated with and appear no different from the other people marching. The protesters and the filmmakers encounter teargas used against them by authorities.

> The work occurred within the protest and is not a work about the protest. The title, *This Lemon Tastes of Apple*, refers to the use of gas against Kurdish people in a genocide attempt. When, in 1988, Saddam's forces were pouring suffocating gas into Halabja and other Kurdish settlements, the gas had a smell of apple. The smell has since had a strong association in the political memory of the country. During the recent months of demonstrations, the people of Kurdistan were attacked by teargas, deployed by their own Kurdish regional government. To relieve the impact of the gas the protesters used lemon as an immediate detoxifying agent. The fruity smells connect the two ends of this 23-year-long history.
>
> (Hiwa K 2011)

These examples raise critical questions concerning the ways that the performance frame might be hinted at, given away, or made legible. Frames can provoke shifts in perception that amplify and explore questions of separateness: What is in or out, what is real or false, what is known or unknown and by whom, who is doing what to whom? Legibility regarding the differentiations of frames, and nested frames, becomes complicated and sometimes contested for viewers (Turner, Turner 1982). In the film *End of*

Life, characters perform acts of their own life through shifting frames, both making clear and obscuring their self-reflective proximity to dying. This tension is transferred to film viewers in ways that ideally support their own reflective practice and expands ways for learning and knowing in regard to their mortality.

The process for mapping the machinations of identity formation—the activities of identifying what's inside or outside of the boundaries that define a person, group, thing, or other formations of organization—is another kind of *design dramaturgy*.

The desire to belong and the potential power of collective belonging are strange bedfellows for the individual and their sense of identity. Are we defined by the group, or does our behavior define the group? Gleaning insights through utilizing performance and frames of expression can be useful for identifying potential leverage points within complex systems. Collective practices for social transformation often confront thorny issues that can divide people according to differing positions, opinions, beliefs, stakes, histories, traumas, and so forth. The characterizing nodes of these complex systems can be psychological, social, geographic, economic, philosophical, spiritual, and more.

The *End of Life* project experimented with design dramaturgy to explore forms of image-oriented reflective practice concerning issues of identity and identification. In addition to the film *End of Life*, other inquiries utilized combinations of recorded and live performance in collaboration with Matthew Freedman, for example, the short film *ACME Death Kit*, as part of the installation/performance (IM)MORTALITY. The first few minutes of *ACME Death Kit* feature a black screen with the sound of Freedman delivering a performance. He retells a joke by Groucho Marx, "A man facing execution by hanging steps onto the platform of the gallows, and says, 'I don't think this thing is very safe'" (Bruce, Wojtasik 2018). As the film continues, Matt appears, and utilizing one of his typical modes of performance, he tells stories while drawing on a large pad of paper hanging from around his neck, as shown in Figure 3.3. He renders images illustrating anecdotes that alternate between humorous, random factoids and his very real experiences with a terminal illness. In another scene, he appears wearing a Lucha libre mask while playing the cello, as shown in Figure 3.3. The film ends with him walking off camera, off the screen. In the Park Place Gallery where we showed the film as part of the installation (IM)MORTALITY, Matt appears from down a darkened hallway, stepping in front of the live audience in perfect synchronization with his body as it disappeared from the film screen, as shown in the images in Figure 3.4. At this moment during the event, there was an audible gasp followed by laughter from the audience. Matt continues the story about his terminal illness, making live drawings on the

Figure 3.3 Matthew Freedman performing in the film *ACME Death Kit*, making drawings and playing the cello in a Lucha libre mask, 2018.

Figure 3.4 Matthew Freedman performing during the (IM)MORTALITY installation, along with the screening of the film *ACME Death Kit*, Park Place Gallery, 2018.

pad around his neck, and then tosses the paper aside, lifts up his shirt, and draws directly on his bare chest. During this moment of the performance, Matt tells a story about the radiation treatments that targeted the tumors in his lungs, and the tattoo marks for aiming the beams. Matt's drawings and stories segue to metaphorically visualize a battlefield on the surface of and within his body. These uses of marks and screens are devices for identifying experiences of mortality that serve to both free and implicate Matt Freedman as a human being and a body navigating the characteristics of a terminal illness. Strategies of design dramaturgy can provide experiences for audiences to travel along with narrative journeys—to participate in the frame slippages afforded by a broken fourth wall through the permeability of boundaries. This experiment, and others, provides insights for designing participatory processes that can bridge distances that entrench separateness, in this case separating from the consciousness of one's mortality. These distances, in turn, can often separate the dying from realms of compassionate and caring spaces of social exchange and belonging.

Masks have long played a major role in dramatic performances. These devices have been utilized as forms of character expression from ancient Greece, Roman commedia dell'arte, Japanese Noh and Kabuki, Balinese Wayang Kulit shadow puppets, Amazon Indian dance masks, and Tibetan mystery plays to contemporary comic superheroes, and more. Performance traditions of masking and the 'body as mask' are rich and vast, while too expansive to be fully examined in this discussion. However, it is worth considering examples, as above, and others, where masking the body serves as a design dramaturgy to break the fourth wall within transdisciplinary approaches. These can be intricate and effective strategies of appearance and disappearance, potentiality and impotentiality, for opening up spaces for education in movement. A potent example is the masked image of the members of the Zapatista movement in Mexico, along with the particular narrative forms of their communiques. Subcomandante Marcos is formerly the spokesperson for the Zapatista Army of National Liberation (EZLN) and the iconic figurehead of the movement who always appeared in a ski mask and often smoking a pipe. Communiques from the EZLN were often unusual in their tone—lyrical, humorously poetic, or familiar. They sometimes were issued as fable forms of narrative, often in conversation with a beetle named Durito, and served as a way to code-switch between political rhetoric and cultural ways of being (Conant 2010). The name Subcomandante Marcos is also a mask—a nom de guerre, attempting not to hide but to diminish the individual in service to the collective, ideally so that the movement lives beyond the confines of one person in terms of both mortal longevity and identifying characteristics. Marcello Tari, in his book *There Is No Unhappy Revolution: The Communism of Destitution*, illuminates these strategies in terms of revolutionary movements as being *destituent* gestures (Tari 2021).

It thus falls to one's own self to dissolve the ego along with the enemy reality during the process of a revolutionary becoming. This self-destitution of the militant simultaneously consists of: allowing for the deception of one's own social identity; the deactivation of the tool of ideology; and, grasping the power of the mask, of that particular mode of existing that is militancy itself. It is a form of life one undertakes by performing a very particular relation to one's own role and to the world, founded on the commitment to truth – the truth of that encounter which everyone experiences in their lifetime, not with any particular person or idea, but with force.

(Tari 2021, p. 5)

Tari states that the destituent gesture moves in the inverse of gestures that are constituent, referencing Benjamin,

Decisive as the masses are for the revolutionary leader, therefore, his great achievement lies not in drawing the masses after him, but in constantly incorporating himself into the masses, in order to be, for them, always one among hundreds of thousands.

(Benjamin [1935] (2008), cited in Tari 2021, p. 144)

Ram Dass is not using a mask in the video that features him staring without speaking, while his presentation obscures identity in ways that invite deeper participation of audiences through their senses. Having been born as Richard Alpert, he was given the name Ram Dass, meaning to serve God in 1967 by Hindu guru Neem Karoli Baba after leaving his jet-setting lifestyle as a Harvard Professor and son of a very wealthy New England family (Ram Dass [1971] 1978). He gained a great deal of public recognition through serving for decades as a spiritual teacher, appearing in several films, and as the author of the best-selling book, *Be Here Now*. However, the last teaching sessions he conducted before his death in December 2019, as collected in a feature-length film, are called *Becoming Nobody*. While I was present with Ram Dass, during our fieldwork with the *End of Life* project, he told me that he was not Ram Dass. He told me that Ram Dass is some guy walking up ahead of him—a figure—that he could barely see from many yards behind, as he followed while becoming nobody. And if he does have a name, perhaps it is something like *soul one*. When I tell this story to students at Parsons, it is often met with strange combinations of trepidation and delight. One group of graduate students in the Transdisciplinary Design program launched, along with me, an artistic-based research project to explore these questions:

We propose that this reliance on historicized, abstract representations perpetuates siloed understandings of self and other, reinforces hierarchical and contentious relations, and limits creative explorations of intersubjectivity. Could we use clothing and film maximally, as sensuous mediators to disrupt and potentially reveal entrenched processes of identification in discourse? How might the affordances of clothing and film be used to mask visual signifiers of identity and activate a viewer's body through textures, sound, colors?

(Bruce et al. 2021)

They made a series of short films, *Identity/Identification*, featuring conversations among small groups that they had 'masked' in clothing, cosmetics, and accessories. These films were shown to audiences to spur discursive exchanges for examining the effects of visual bias on the 'legibility' of discourse. Preliminary findings from this research indicate that disruptions in visual identity markers foster a shift in the qualities of attention paid toward the content of discussions.

Herein lie the core issues around the collective as it takes shape through the participation of individuals. These are notions and gestures of potentiality and impotentiality, legibility and illegibility, renaming to identify behaviors and to prevent tendencies that conflate essentialism with identity politics, and for inviting contributions to the conditions that promote atmospheres for the emergence of collective effervescence toward collective liberation.

Reflection exercise

I have shown the film *Charlie Pisuk*, described above, to several groups of graduate students of the Transdisciplinary Design program at Parsons, sometimes without any introduction to the film's collaborative origins or conceptual form. On one occasion, this 'cold open' presentation resulted in a collective reaction that began from one student's response to the film as an abusive display—they had taken the narrative at face-value and empathetically suffered heart-break for the characters. The student's emotional response spread to others, and soon there was a chorus of angry comments directed at the film and at me for having shown it. When I asked if they could describe the *form* of the film they had just experienced, only a critique of the content was offered. After a short amount of time, and as I feared groupthink had taken over their critical capacities, I disclosed that *Charlie Pisuk* was a hybrid film of (non)fiction. This revelation triggered several surprising reactions. First, some students were angry, perhaps a defense of experiencing embarrassment at having been hood-winked by the film, and in turn placed culpability on me for having not disclosed the film's fictional and collaborative aspects in advance. These students felt deep discomfort and expressed their objection—a dual rejection of confrontation. Other students deemed the fictional and collaborative frame of the film as inconsequential to the triggering effects of witnessing Indigenous people being subjected to an oppressive force. While none of the students was Native American, First Nations, or Indigenous, one student was emotionally distraught, spurring other students to join this position in a moment of classroom solidarity.

This particular group's reaction to viewing *Charlie Pisuk* raised critical questions around the politics of helping and the proliferation of narratives of damage. While uncomfortable for everyone, as a learning community we were able to leverage the experience and gain important capacities for reflection and reading performance frames. The empowered position of the characters appearing in *Charlie Pisuk* is made legible through a sophisticated use of the performance of ethnography as an act of anti-ethnography. The film is a rich example of participatory artistic- and design-based research and serves as an effective design provotype. The class comprised students who were only a few weeks into their graduate education, having enrolled in a program focused on transdisciplinary research and design approaches for addressing complex social issues. Many students arrive at the program with entrenched ideas that conflate notions of social transformation with helping. These students might be too quick to read narratives as damaging, and for understandable reasons. Research artifacts gathered through observations of communities that are challenged by conditions of oppression, disenfranchisement, and other damaging forces are prolific. These research engagements can reinforce negative community impressions and reflections through continuous cycles of investigations that perpetually yield damage-focused narratives (Tuck 2009). This kind of hyper-legibility can obscure other, potentially opportunistic, dimensions of a community. Eve Tuck suggests modes for learning that suspend narratives of damage and alternatively embrace desire-based research frameworks—approaches that are "concerned with understanding complexity, contradiction, and the self-determination of lived lives" (Tuck 2009, p. 416). Desire-based research frameworks raise ideas around hybrid and prefigurative narratives that might propose models for reaching forward—embodying and performing—as movements within future trajectories. Tuck cites Craig Gingrich-Philbrook's example of the need for desire-based frameworks, referencing the historical tendency for narratives about the same-sex relationship to focus on pain and pathos and never including a same-sex kiss (Gingrich-Philbrook 2005, cited in Tuck 2009). Gran Fury, the artist and designer affinity group within ACT-UP, launched a series of bus advertisements in New York City in the early 1990s featuring same-sex and mixed-race configurations of kissing couples, with the tagline "Kissing Doesn't Kill: Greed and Indifference Do" (Gran Fury 1989). At the time, seeing these images move through New York City was brilliantly moving.

Charlie Pisuk functions as a participatory research framework to center Indigenous experiences and expressions through co-creative reflection, critical design, and performing ethnography as anti-ethnography. However, readings of the film that lack capacities for recognizing its performance frame strategy might default to perceptions of entrenched damage narratives and reify, albeit unwittingly and accidentally, racist positions. The insights gleaned from experiences with *Charlie Pisuk* served as an opportunity to consider how we, as a learning community, might build capacities for seeing and working with performance frames. A subset of students from the class along with the teaching team designed an exercise in response to the discussions surrounding *Charlie Pisuk* and other similar examples of performed ethnography and performance frames. The Reflection Exercise, below, outlines an experience for exploring issues of disclosure, implicit bias, and non-preconception in an effort for building capacities around deep listening, watching closely, reflection, and understanding performance frames.

REFLECTION EXERCISE, OUTLINE OF ACTIVITIES

Each participant is given a copy of one of the six descriptions (seedings) framing the video that they are about to watch. Each seeding is different, and all are accurate. Participants are informed that the video is almost seven minutes in duration and are given no other information.

The video features Ram Dass, who had been a spiritual teacher, author, and university professor. The video image, as described in detail in Chapter 1, Images or Crisis, Images of Change, shows Ram Dass in a medium close-up shot, staring directly into the camera. He seems to be about to speak but hesitates. He occasionally strokes his beard, clears his throat, and tilts his head. At one moment, he sips water from a glass. Sounds that are heard in the video, at certain moments, include an airplane passing overhead, chimes, and birdsong. Near the end of the video, Ram Dass says, "In our culture, almost everybody is afraid of death." The video does not display any titles, captions, or credits.

Outline of activities

- Issue one seeding per participant (no seeding for a few)
- After everyone privately reads their seeding, all watch the video
- Gather in discussion groups based, either homogenous or mixed according to seedings
- Share the prompt questions (below). Groups discuss for 10 minutes

After ten minutes of discussion among participants within the small, numbered groups, all participants are reconvened as one large group. Representatives from the breakout groups are asked to share highlights from their discussions. After this collective round of share-back, all six seedings are read aloud to everyone, followed by the question: How might we as design researchers navigate notions of disclosure, implicit bias, and efforts of non-preconception in our processes?

Seeding 01: The subject of this film clip was born to a Jewish Family in Newton, Massachusetts, in 1931. His father was a prominent lawyer, served as President of the New York, New Haven and Hartford Railroad and was one of the founders of Brandeis University and the Albert Einstein College of Medicine. The subject received an undergraduate degree from Tufts, a master's degree from Wesleyan and a PhD from Stanford University, all in psychology, and became a tenure track professor at Harvard teaching and conducting research within the Social Relations Department, the Psychology Department, and the Graduate School of Education.

Seeding 02: The subject of this film clip suffered a stroke in 1997 that left him suffering from expressive aphasia (a type of aphasia that makes speech effortful although it typically doesn't affect comprehension).

Seeding 03: The subject of this film clip co-authored the books *The Psychedelic Experience* based on *The Tibetan Book of the Dead* and LSD, both published in the mid-1960s and both of which chronicled many experiments with hallucinatory drugs such as LSD and psilocybin ingested in the pursuit of 'a permanent route to higher consciousness.'

Seeding 04: The subject of this film clip was fired from his tenure track professorship at Harvard University for allegedly giving psilocybin to an undergraduate. He was a noted drug user who experimented extensively with psychedelic drugs throughout the 60s and 70s.

Seeding 05: The subject of this film clip is Ram Dass, noted spiritual teacher and author of the spiritual bestseller *Be Here Now* which has remained in print since it was published in 1971 and has sold over 2 million copies. He donated the proceeds of the book to the non-profit Hanuman foundation which is focused on the spiritual well-being of society through education, media, and community service programs. He has donated all his earnings from teaching and writing (estimated to be between 100,000 and 800,000 dollars a year) to support the foundation and other spiritually supportive institutions.

Seeding 06: The filmmakers approached Ram Dass about the ongoing development of a project with aims to be present with people at various stages of the end of life. The filmmakers met with Ram Dass and discussed the project before any recording commenced. On the first day of filming, lengthy discussions were recorded. On subsequent days, a co-creative approach to experimentation was discussed. The first experiment was for all to meditate together, including the cameras—meaning they were on but not manipulated during meditation, for 12 minutes. After this exercise, the filmmakers asked Ram Dass to guide a journey regarding the mystery of contemplating mortality and to consider how dispositions of fear and anxiety might be guided to places of grace and peace. It was offered that such guidance might include words, or not, and might include other expressions, gestures, or considerations of being present.

Possible prompt questions for discussion

In what ways, if any, were you interested in hearing what the subject had to say?

How might you describe any opinions about the subject that arose for you while watching the film clip?

What physical details did you notice about the subject while watching the film? In noticing these, did you form any opinions around the subject?

In what ways, if any, did you experience empathy toward the subject while watching the film clip?

Far from Nauru

An odd war of appearances seems to be escalating that compounds the challenges for affective transitions toward greater sustainability. Thresholds often appear like mirages—illusionary, hyper-legible images that misdirect attention for identifying leverage points. The catastrophic events resulting from the climate crisis produce startling images. These are important to see and can also be instrumentalized in ways that appear as warped traces and obscure the legibility for potential paths forward. For anyone living in a media-connected world, it might be hard to miss these images: polar bears seemingly stranded on tiny chunks of ice, massive fires that scorch miles of landscape and devastate lives, freakish flash floods, and so on. Science, and now common sense, confirms these calamities as the result of climate change brought about through our presence as humans and the systems we have created. The scale of these systems as related to our human scale of perception create great distances—enormous expanses of time and space to traverse in order to make decisions and take actions—for movements to reach thresholds of transition and transformation. Building new capacities to see within, across, and beyond that which is and is not seeable requires new kinds of narrative literacies for visualizing in performative, contextual, bespoke, fluid, and uncertain ways.

Long ago in a land far, far away. This is a story that might seem like fiction, yet came to my attention through an article that appeared in the Sunday *New York Times* on December 10, 1995. The article's headline reads: "A Pacific Island Nation is Stripped of Everything." A photograph of the barren landscape of Nauru shows a field of otherworldly rock formations, with a caption that reads:

> There wasn't much to start with and now, after 90 years of strip-mining, almost nothing is left of the tiny Pacific island of Nauru. The islanders, plagued by a bad diet and low life expectancy, may have to move.
>
> (Shenon 1995)

At the time of the article's publication, the 7,500 people of Nauru were among the wealthiest in the world. The island's rich deposits of phosphate in the form of guano—the result of millions of years of migratory birds stopping by on this eight-square mile spot of land in the middle of the Pacific Ocean—was mined and exported for large profits. Two other images appear with the article: a photograph of a group of overweight Nauruans holding softball mitts; and, a map showing the island's location in the Pacific, about a third of the way between Australia and Hawaii. The hyper-reality of this narrative as prompted by the images, headline, and caption produces intrigue that seduces more than informs. The article's opening line is akin to that of a parable:

> Even the most diligent map-maker might be excused for overlooking this tiny wind-buffeted island – a spit of sand and coral hidden in an obscure stretch of the western Pacific, a place literally close to nowhere.
>
> (Shenon 1995)

The journalistic details are both dark and oddly delightful. The images of Nauru and the Nauruans in the *New York Times* article charge the speculation that *the islanders may have to move* with the essence of a dystopian fairytale far, far away and draws the reader into a swirl of wonder regarding the causality that might have brought about such a precarious future. The photo of the Nauruans, overweight, on the beach with their softball mitts—is an indicting portrait. Life expectancy is under 60 years of age for most islanders due to obesity and diabetes from a poor diet, "Nauruans stopped farming decades ago when, with the easy income from phosphate, they discovered the convenience of shipped-in canned and frozen foods. For most, a traditional diet of fresh fish and vegetables has been replaced by Spam, canned corned beef, potato chips and beer" (Shenon 1995). The article reports that the Nauruans have an enormous trust fund that is a constant target for scams. Millions invested and lost in a failed London-based musical theater production based on the life of Leonardo da Vinci, "Not coincidentally, the musical, 'Leonardo, Portrait of Love,' was co-written by one of the country's British financial advisers" (Shenon 1995).

Colonization by Germany, Japan, and, predominantly, Australia, along with strip-mining, plagued the island since the late 19th century. The Nauruans, having gained independence in 1968, continued strip-mining phosphate, becoming incredibly rich, only to discover that the mine would soon be depleted. The island's ecosystem for sustaining crops had been destroyed from land degradation and also climate change—the result of heat-island effect from the rocky, barren landscape that now comprised a large proportion of the island's interior. At the time of the 1995 *New York Times* article, Nauru's leaders were considering spending down their trust on either replenishing the topsoil in an attempt to grow crops or buying a new island and moving (Shenon 1995). The information in the article functions with a kind of narrative slipperiness, shifting attention from human experiences to grand systems, and back again. What might an event of forced migration—abandoning an island—look like for 7,500 people with great wealth? The situation is made legible by way of parameters at odd scales. The narrative seems to pose questions that frame the predicament as perhaps manageable, merely requiring a decision, despite the dire stakes at hand.

The 1995 story of Nauru as it appeared in the *New York Times* is perhaps a kind of mapping legend for what was a burgeoning popular awareness, at that time, around the unsustainable conditions of the planet as brought about by humans and more specifically colonization and late capitalism. Four-fifths of Nauru had been mined resulting in a sunbaked terrain that changed weather patterns and reduced rainfall, resulting in frequent drought (Shenon 1995).

The rise of neoliberal attitudes and global policy trends have elevated ideological narratives of individual responsibility. Despite proximities enabled by technology, distances that 'other' prevail and posit the responsibility of tragedy on the individual—ignoring the complexity of systemic conditions. Cautionary tales, from *Silent Spring*, Rachel Carson's 1964 book calling out the dangers of pesticides, to Nauru, are narratives that serve in important ways for sounding alarms. At the same time, certain forms of narrative legibility can also entrench notions that dystopian scenarios will remain far from us, the same way that fables tend to include the comfort of safe distances. After all, chronic bee colony collapse has persisted for many years, even as compelling narratives have linked certain pesticides to this tragedy. Bees pollinate crops and are essential to the food chain. Despite a ban in 2018 by the European Union on the use of neonicotinoid pesticides, based on studies connecting colony collapse to these chemicals, loopholes allow their continued use (Clarke, Dowler 2020). Watchdog organization Greenpeace reports that the counter narratives supporting these loopholes are framed as "emergency authorisations"—instances where the use of these pesticides is the only way to address imminent dangers to farming or ecological systems, while the rationales for claiming such emergencies are often market-driven logics and have little to do with farming or environmental stewardship (Clarke, Dowler 2020). For example, one of the awarded petitions for 'emergency authorization' was from a golf course (Clarke, Dowler 2020).

From a distance, seeing and hearing the Nauruans occurs through vivid traces as reported in the *New York Times* article. This appearance functions in ways—much more than merely hinting—to directly connect the unfolding tragedy of their existence to global and indictable forces. Despite this compelling narrative supported by striking photographs, Nauru's plight appears as an abstraction to the degree that accountability remains untethered. The situated predicaments of the Nauruans and the bees fail to be expressed in ways that might reverse perspectives that cast their reality as abstracted within neoliberal regimes of deterritorialization. By no means am I intending any criticisms of the reporting cited in this discussion, as these efforts are indeed professionally sound and worthy. Stories like the devastation of Nauru and bee colony collapse point to what might be the demands and opportunities for new ways to pay attention.

> What we have been ordered to forget is not the capacity to pay attention, but the art of paying attention. If there is an art, and not just a capacity, this is because it is a matter of learning and cultivating, that is to say, making ourselves pay attention. Making in the sense that attention here is not related to that which is defined as a priori worthy of attention, but as something that creates an obligation to imagine,

to check, to envisage, consequences that bring into play connections between what we are in the habit of keeping separate.

(Stengers 2015, p. 62)

Separateness can derail the momentum and direction of movements toward change. The story of the island of Nauru provides rapier-sharp perspectives on issues of sustainability reflecting the island's history with colonization, a globalized economy, and deterritorialization, while a threshold of movement cannot be bridged in these ways alone. Nauru or the Nauruans are not the problem or the solution. Systems of interdependence can become camouflaged within symptoms of striking calamities rendered as broad narratives. The January 3 and 10, 2022, issue of *The New Yorker* magazine includes an article about the immanent possibility of seabed mining and cites Nauru as the linchpin dictating the timetable for the start of this environmentally destructive activity (Kolbert 2021). The article, by Pulitzer Prize-winning journalist and author Elizabeth Kolbert, sketches a brief, somewhat flattening description of Nauru as having "a long history of disastrous business dealings," and having been, "administered by Australia," before attaining independence in 1968 (Kolbert 2021). I intend no disrespect for Kolbert and indeed agree that seabed mining must be stopped. While I cannot see the value in demonizing Nauru, just as I do not believe that jailing the addict solves the opioid crisis. The particular scale of a complex system is intertwined with the capacity to perceive the fulsome dimensions of situations, and their histories with dependence, independence, and interdependence, especially those regarding issues of sustainability.

The complexity of both the calamities and cautionary tales as gleaned through the stories regarding Nauru and bee colony collapse are salient examples for making the case for participation as a more effective way for co-creating and sharing critical knowledge—whether through the performance of ethnography and frames of expressions or other forms of embodied learning—toward movements of transformation. The capacities to grapple with— the art of paying attention to—challenging situations of great scale and from great distances are contingent on access to sensory engagements often requiring encounters beneath the surface of didactic narratives. How might we sense the global population, its existence, its growth, its interdependence?

Reverberating narratives and transdisciplinarity

The term *movement* is used in this chapter to intentionally provoke imaginative interpretations of the ways participatory research and design might instigate change—move things. Certainly, movement can be thought of in terms of social movements, and efforts thereof, for example, design of new programs, services, policy, systems: movement toward safe and available food, water, and housing; movement toward prison abolition; movement toward carbon neutrality; movement toward healthcare as a right; and movement toward other issues and initiatives on a very long list of matters regarding equity, inclusion, and social, economic, and environmental justice. Movement is also engaging in the consciousness of tensions—anticipation—that expands sensibilities before actions might unfold. These are spaces where opportunities for sense-making and decision-making can inform collective movement with greater momentum and traction. Learning how to best exploit these spaces requires reflective practices to inform collective, embodied, visceral visions toward thresholds—ways to move together, *becoming with*.

Transdisciplinary research takes place in fluid constellations of participatory interactions. These spaces are brought about through acts of convening stakeholders and creating conditions that support a myriad of functions for seekers and sharers. Transdisciplinary spaces might resemble versions of an ancient Greek *agora*—a central gathering place for citizens to play, perform, create, debate, compete, and exchange in a variety of ways, located adjacent to structures housing democratic processes for participatory governance and administration (Lang et al. 2004). The agora, as positioned adjacent to or nested within complimentary community infrastructures, is a model for transdisciplinary research hubs that seek to facilitate the creation of new knowledge through a diversity of participatory engagements.

The idea of agora might also exist virtually or temporarily—shift like pop-ups or Bedouin Tents—and serve as enclosures that remain open, a kind of commons. An agora might be a transition hub like a pirate's cove—a secret perch from which to launch *pirate acts* for hacking, circumventing, and queering systems of containment and oppression (Halberstam 2011). The prefix 'trans' meaning 'across' or 'beyond' can also refer to movement *to the other side* (trans 2010). The German expression *anderes Ufer* is translated as the *other shore*, or *other bank*, and is also an idiomatic expression that connotes queerness (Schemann, Knight 1995). José Esteban Muñoz thinks of "queerness as a temporal arrangement in which the past is a field of possibility in which subjects can act in the present in the service of a new futurity" (Muñoz 2009, p. 16). Not coincidentally, the first openly gay and lesbian café in Germany, established in 1977, was named Anderes Ufer (Lange 2016). Instead of operating in the shadows—behind heavy curtains or unmarked entrances, as was the case for gay and lesbian gatherings places, Anderes Ufer celebrated its presence as a beacon of queer visibility and an open invitation to the other side. I spent many long afternoons at Anderes Ufer in Berlin during the summer of 1986, in the weeks before my 22nd birthday. My patronage was social and also motivated by a dire need for sources of knowledge to help me navigate life as a queer person in a world where stigmas were prevalent, especially within an atmosphere of great uncertainty and crisis brought about by the advent and impacts of HIV/AIDS. Jeremy Atherton Lin's book, *Gay Bar: Why We Went Out*, provides historical and auto-ethnographic accounts of several queer establishments in various cities, illuminating the ways these spaces simultaneously functioned as hubs for resistance, sourcing information, bonding, and celebrating to evolve queer consciousness. Lin quotes historian John D'Emilio who wrote about queer establishments that emerged after the Second World War as, "Alone among expressions of gay life, the bar fostered an identity that was both public and collective" (D'Emilio 1983, cited in Lin 2021, p. 128).

HIV/AIDS, during the 1980s, cast a bright light on the ways that the interdependence of social systems can be extremely valuable and precarious, indeed similar to insights gleaned during the Covid-19 pandemic. These kinds of crises can spur sudden shifts in ethical perspectives and cast existing structures as legible in new ways. Family ties, support for frontline workers, judgments fueled by political or cultural ideologies, and other issues and relationships are often rendered in high relief during a crisis. Information needed to make sense of troubling and confusing times might be hard to find, and its fidelity might raise skepticism or foster suspicion of trust. Finding my way to Anderes Ufer in Berlin in 1986 is an example of my naive (and fortuitous) mode of embodied learning through participation in multicultural knowledge domains. I was visiting Berlin from the East Village of Manhattan where I lived, at that time, among a community of people and places that invited camaraderie *on the other side*—ways of being that circumvented conservative social norms and invented ad hoc configurations of solidarity for exploration, expression, and survival. The East Village hosted places that served as temporal agoras, made manifest by activists, artists, anarchists, squatters, and a host of other queering seekers and sharers through the appropriation of abandoned buildings and public parks for social, art, and political gatherings. Anderes Ufer and hundreds of similar spaces around the world functioned to support conditions for exchange where lay people served equally, if not more so, as experts and authorities in gathering, translating, and synthesizing information from a wide range of sources and contexts. Certain groups who were, and still are today, disproportionally impacted by HIV/AIDS—gay men, intravenous drug users, people of color, and people economically disenfranchised— were the impetus for and agents of a movement that rose to fill an egregious gap in knowledge. They labored collectively to create paths for transformation, motivated by stakes of life or death, as directly stated in the opening paragraph of Sarah Schulman's book *Let the Record Show: A Political History of ACT UP New York, 1987–1993*:

> This is the story of a despised group of people, with no rights, facing a terminal disease for which there were no treatments. Abandoned by their families, government, and society, they joined together and forced our country to change against its will, permanently impacting future movements of people with AIDS throughout the world and saving incalculable numbers of future lives. Some men and women with AIDS fought until the day they died. The dead and the living ultimately transformed the crisis
>
> (Schulman 2021, p. 23)

The actions, past and present, of ACT UP and other advocacy and activist groups, as illuminated through Schulman's book and several other books, documentary films, exhibitions, and ongoing events, serve as powerful models for transdisciplinary praxis, especially as supported by image-oriented narratives. These examples range from the above-cited *Kissing Doesn't Kill* campaign designed by Gran Fury to intricately orchestrated and visually compelling acts of civil disobedience. Several of these actions utilized 'die-ins'—a form of protest simulating being dead, demanding confrontation and disrupting 'business as usual' in churches, in front of government agencies, and in the middle of roadways. Slogans and signage featured bracing imagery, for example, a bloody handprint with text, "THE GOVERNMENT HAS BLOOD ON ITS HANDS—ONE AIDS DEATH EVERY HALF HOUR" (Gran Fury 1988). These kinds of images were designed to attract the attention of news media cameras and in turn be widely circulated. Controlling the narrative in these ways effectively redirected attention away from images of victimhood and served to elevate—make legible—HIV/AIDS through urgent issues and arguments: faster development of treatment and prevention, public policy to support people living with HIV/AIDS, dispelling harmful misinformation, and other critical matters. It also created conditions that focused the cultural conversation and forced the public to confront the complex realities of the crisis.

The war of appearances rages on in the United States of America, by the United States of America. A quote often attributed, while not confirmed, to Joseph Stalin, "a single death is a tragedy, a million deaths are a statistic," speaks to the question of proximity and the art of paying attention. Certainly, both examples, one death and a million deaths, are tragic. Over time, the quote has become politically charged with the intention of rightfully shaming Americans for their tendency to see tragedy in war as only those (certain) Americans who die while the countless (often literally uncounted) deaths of others are framed in dehumanizing ways (Tirman 2015). There are several movements, from suffrage and civil rights to the Black Panther Party, the Zapatistas, and others, that have leveraged image-oriented narratives and performance expressions in ways that can serve as valuable examples to learn from. Black Lives Matter calls attention to an America that cannot see Black Americans, too often does not count Black Americans, and kills Black Americans. Black Lives Matter is a movement that effectively mobilizes narratives and performance through collective visualization, making thresholds legible, and manifesting transformations for equity and justice. Participatory artistic- and design-based research to serve efforts of social transformation requires a constant forge of moving toward thresholds—learning through making, embodied sensing and reflecting, educating in movement, and becoming together.

References

Agamben, G. (1999) *Potentialities: Collected Essays in Philosophy*, Redwood City, CA: Stanford University Press.

Akama, Y. (2015) Being Awake to *Ma*: Designing in Between-Ness as a Way of Becoming with. *CoDesign* 11(3–4), pp. 262–274.

Arnait Video (Film Producers) (2015) *Charlie Pisuk*, Arnait Video Productions. Retrieved from http://www.isuma.tv/en/arnaitvideo/charlie-pisuk.

Benjamin, W. (2008 [1935]) The Work of Art in the Age of its Technical Reproducibility. In Michael W. Jennings, Brigid Doherty, Thomas Y. Levin, eds. *The Work of Art in the Age of its Technical Reproducibility and Other Writings on Media*, Cambridge, MA and London: Belknap Press, p. 50.

Bruce, J.A., Huang, D., Tran, A., Faedo, G. (2021) *Identity/Identification*, unpublished research.

Bruce, J.A., Wojtasik, P. (Directors) (2017) *End of Life*, US: Grasshopper Films.

Bruce, J.A., Wojtasik, P. (Directors) (2017) *End of Life*, US: Grasshopper Films. Reflection Exercise excerpt, retrieved from https://vimeo.com/269308911.

Bruce, J.A., Wojtasik, P. (Directors) (2018) *ACME Death Kit (Motion Picture Film, 2018), Installation and Performance, (IM)MORTALITY*, New York: Park Place Gallery, May.

Clarke, J., Dower, C. (2020) Loophole Keeps Bee-Killing Pesticides in Widespread Use, Two Years after EU Ban. *UNEARTHED*, July 8. Retrieved from https://unearthed.greenpeace.org/2020/07/08/bees-neonicotinoids-bayer-syngenta-eu-ban-loophole/.

Conant, J. (2010) *A Poetics of Resistance: The Revolutionary Public Relations of the Zapatista Insurgency*, Oakland, CA: AK Press.

Delany, S.R. (1996 [1975]) *Dhalgren*, New York: Bantam Books, Inc. New England: Wesleyan University Press.

D'Emilio, J. (1983) *Sexual Politics, Sexual Communities: The Making of a Homosexual Minority in the United States 1940–1970*, Chicago: University of Chicago Press.

Douglas, M. (1980 [1966]) *Purity and Danger: An Analysis of Concepts of Pollution and Taboo*, New York, NY: Routledge & Kegan Paul.

Douglas, M. (1984 [1966]) *Purity and Danger: An Analysis of Concepts of Pollution and Taboo*, ARK ed., Routledge & Kegan Paul.

Gingrich-Philbrook, C. (2005) Autoethnography's Family Values. *Text and Performance Quarterly* 25(4), pp. 297–314.

Goffman, E. (1986) *Frame Analysis: An Essay on the Organization of Experience*, Boston: Northeastern University Press.

Gran Fury (1988) Manuscripts and Archives Division, The New York Public Library. *The Government Has Blood on Its Hands. One AIDS Death Every Half Hour*. Retrieved from https://digitalcollections.nypl.org/items/510d47e3-3ebe-a3d9-e040-e00a18064a99.

Gran Fury (Artist collective) (1989) *Kissing Doesn't Kill: Greed and Indifference Do*, Creative Time: New York City. Retrieved from https://creativetime.org/projects/kissing-doesnt-kill-greed-and-indifference-do/.

Halberstam, J. (2011) *The Queer Art of Failure*, Durham: Duke University Press.

Hiwa K (2011) *This Lemon Tastes of Apple*, Retrieved from www.hiwak.net.

Institute of Radical Imagination (IRI) (2021) [website], Retrieved from https://instituteofradicalimagination.org/mission-and-values/.

Isuma.TV (2021) Available online: http://www.isuma.tv/arnaitvideo/charlie-pisuk

Kolbert, E. (2021) Mining the Bottom of the Sea: The Future of the Largest, Still Mostly Untouched Ecosystem in the World is at Risk. *The New Yorker*, December 26. Published in the print edition of the January 3 & 10, 2022, issue, with the headline "In Deep." Retrieved from https://www.newyorker.com/magazine/2022/01/03/mining-the-bottom-of-the-sea.

Kondylatou, D. (2020) Confined Spaces. In David Bergé, Dimitra Kondylatou, Nicolas Lakiotakis, eds. *Public Health in Crisis: Confined in the Aegean Archipelago*, Athens: Kyklàda Press, pp. 17–59.

Lang, M., Camp, J.M.K., Frantz, A. (2004) *The Athenian Citizen: Democracy in the Athenian Agora*, Princeton: American School of Classical Studies at Athens.

Lange, N. (2016) "Café Neues Ufer in Berlin-Schoeneberg: Palm trees, stars and roses" *Der Tagesspiegel*, August 8, 2016.

Latour, B. (2005) *Reassembling the Social: An Introduction to Actor-Network Theory*, Oxford: Oxford University Press.

Lin, J.A.2021) *Gay Bar: Why We Went Out*, New York, NY: Little Brown and Company.

Margulis, L. (1998) *Symbiotic Planet: A New Look at Evolution*, New York: Basic Books.

Mollona, M. (2021) *Art/Commons: Anthropology Beyond Capitalism*, London: Zed Books.

Muñoz, J.E. (2019 [2009]) *Cruising Utopia: The Then and There of Queer Futurity*, New York: New York University Press.

Penin, L. (2018) *An Introduction to Service Design: Designing the Invisible*, London: Bloomsbury.

Ram Dass (1978 [1971]) *Be Here Now*, San Cristobal, New Mexico: Hanuman Foundation.

sacred (2010) *Oxford Dictionary of English*, 2nd ed., Oxford, England: Oxford University Press.

Schemann, P., Knight, P. (1995) anderes ufer. *German-English Dictionary of Idioms: Idiomatik Deutsch English*, New York: Routledge.

Schulman, S. (2021) *Let the Record Show: A Political History of ACT UP New York, 1987–1993*, New York: Farrar, Straus and Giroux.

Sheldrake, M. (2020) *Entangled Life: How Fungi Make Our Worlds, Change Our Minds & Shape Our Futures*, New York: Random House.

Shenon, P. (1995) A Pacific Island Is Stripped of Everything. *New York Times*, December 10.

Stengers, I. (2015) *In Catastrophic Times: Resisting the Coming Barbarism*, London: Open Humanities Press.

Tari, M. (2021) *There Is No Unhappy Revolution: The Communism of Destitution*, Brooklyn, NY: Common Notions.

Tirman, J. (2015) *The Deaths of Others: The Fate of Civilians in America's Wars*, Oxford, England: Oxford University Press.

trans (2010) *Oxford Dictionary of English*, 2nd ed., Oxford, England: Oxford University Press.

Tuck, E. (2009) Suspending Damage: A Letter to Communities. *Harvard Educational Review* 70(3), pp. 409–427.

Turner, E., Turner, V. (1982) Performing Ethnography. *The Drama Review: TDR* 26(2), pp. 33–50. *Intercultural Performance* (Summer, 1982). 1982 by the Massachusetts Institute of Technology.

Zibechi, R. (2012) *Territories in Resistance: A Cartography of Latin American Social Movements*, trans. Ramor Ryan, Oakland, CA: AK Press.

4 Cinematic tropes and designing spectacles

Mary Rossi carried a cardboard box filled with photographs of her life as a child and young woman into the backyard of her home in New Jersey and burned it. She carried out this act alone, sometime in the late 1970s, and told no one at the time. Along with the images of herself, the box contained photos that she had received over several decades from her siblings in Italy. Mary Rossi, my grandmother, was born in 1896 in Atina, Italy, and had emigrated with her husband Carmen to the United States in 1916. She died in 1982. My mother, Elaine Marie Bruce (1939–2011), the second youngest of Mary and Carmen's nine children, told me this story in the early 1990s, during a conversation after having been estranged for many years. Elaine had learned about the burning incident because she had asked her mother if she could have some of the photos. She had worshipped her mother like a saint, yet was confused and wounded by this event. Mary explained that she didn't want her memories stored in anyone's closet. These relationships were hers alone. And as Mary became aware that she was approaching the end of her life, she burned the photographs as a way to honor and keep safe the images and narratives that she had created and shared with people dear to her and who were no longer alive.

In this story, the transit of relational meaning afforded by the materiality of the images had reached its rightful place in the pyre. I imagine that Mary, if she were living today, might provide her rationale for the burning as a gesture to thwart neoliberalism's pernicious coopting of value systems—her photos would not become stock images for selling services for finding one's ancestors, residence in a retirement village, remedies for erectile dysfunction, or any other market-driven lens promoting a preferred lifestyle. My imagination re-enacts the spectacle of Mary's ritual: I see the backyard with the chicken coop at the far end on the right, past the sour apple trees; Mary would have moved slowly, assisted by her cane, toward the slope where she placed kitchen scraps in a compost pile, to the right of the cherry tree I climbed as a child; she might have doused the box with rubbing alcohol she

DOI: 10.4324/9780367365264-4

retrieved from the medicine cabinet that smelled of Mercurochrome; Mary, I wish to believe, did not stand and watch the fire grow with mournful poise, and rather puttered to pick a bunch of ripe grapes or turn over the compost, carrying on with resolute wisdom and quotidian grace. The photographs have disappeared, while these images and narrative remain with me—they have impacted my thoughts and actions over time, contributing to the way I see opportunities and make choices. For me, photography is also an act of love. Spectacles can conjure talismanic gestures that celebrate the transcendental power of images and narratives to shape futures.

Spectacle is defined as a visually striking performance or display, while the phrase 'make a spectacle of oneself' is to draw attention to oneself by behaving in a ridiculous way in public (spectacle 2010). The potential presence of and reception by an audience impacts an event's criteria as a spectacle in curious ways. I was not present, nor was anyone, while my grandmother burned her family photos. However, the retelling of the story functions as a spectacle.

Spectacles can take shape at scales that range from the intimate and personal to the grand and epic. Spectacles, in terms of concept and form, are content agnostic. They can reflect horror or delight, desire or fear, joy or pain, clarity or confusion, and so on. They are narrative *systems* that rely on visually striking performances as elements (variables) to charge relationships and outcomes. For example, I observed, while sitting at a communal dining table at an eco-resort in an isolated stretch of the Oaxaca coast, a young woman struggling with a case of hiccups. The proprietor, an older man and yogi with a showman's flair, served up a remedy, bellowing, "Hold your breath until you are about to die." "Hold it, hold it! Are you dying!?" He waved his arms and pointed a finger almost touching the woman's nose, "hold it!" The woman played along and held her breath for a ridiculous amount of time. I was uncomfortable, watching from the other end of the long table. "Are you about to die," he nearly screamed? She let go of her nose and inhaled. The proprietor's meaty palm slapped the table in front of her, "give me one, give me a hiccup, give me one, now … give it to me, give me one!" Her hiccups were gone. "We need a bit of drama," he said. This event is perhaps a quotidian, even banal, example of dramatic spectacle as compared to, for example, televised events such as NASA's Apollo lunar landings and Janet Jackson's Super Bowl XXXVIII halftime show wardrobe malfunction, or the Nazi propaganda film *Triumph of the Will*. As devices intended to impact an audience—whether to inspire with fantastical new information, shock with surprising turns of events, manipulate beliefs, or a myriad of other affective gestures with the potential to transform—spectacles might be deployed by actors or agents with a multitude of agendas.

Spectacles can play at the epicenter around which other narratives constellate and can also appear as byproducts of larger narratives. As recorded images, they appear in movies as *set pieces* and in daily life on the covers of newspapers. Their sudden emergence is often experienced like a rogue meteorite, wildly accelerating through the atmosphere on a collision-course trajectory with previously held beliefs. Spectacles can occur through the premeditation of produced events, unplanned and unexpected happenings, and a range of combinations thereof. I was five years old and eagerly awaiting Christmas while watching the first televised Selective Service draft lottery on December 1, 1969. The lottery used a system of birth dates assigned to numbers that were contained in capsules and drawn from a bin like a game of bingo. Birth dates in the order drawn from the bin indicated the order by which groups of eligible young men were called to induction into the armed services, and most likely sent to engage in the war taking place in Vietnam. During the televised spectacle, my great uncle Al, always the lovable trickster with a baritone voice, who had been watching with me, dramatically exclaimed, "There it is, your birthday! You're going! You're going to join the war." I spent the next hour in an inconsolable state of hysterical distress. My father's mother, my other grandmother, silently cried along with me. My uncle and the other adults tried to assure me that I was too young, and my father too old, to be drafted, but nevertheless I sobbed without pause, unable to embrace or be soothed by their logics of ineligibility. What these adults failed to realize was that my pathos resulted from my connection to the images I watched every evening on the six o'clock news—black and white 16-mm film footage presenting spectacles of war taking place far away but also close-up, on my TV screen, and as touchable, material objects in my living room. My father's mother was a second-generation Sicilian immigrant. Our houses faced one another, across the street. Several days a week, when she returned home after her workday of sewing zippers into coats in a sweatshop, we cooked food and watched television together. She had a keen sense of observation, street-smarts with a sixth-grade education, and was a joyous and vivacious person, while never painting a pretty picture to cover or deny her feelings of empathy or suffering. Her tearful silence while I cried signaled assurance of and compassion for my painful confrontation with these spectacles of connectedness—that what was happening *there* was happening *here*.

Spectacles can resonate narratively like the light echoes from supernovae. A great deal of attention has been paid to the Selective Service draft lotteries having taken place from 1969 to 1975, in terms of both the impacts on the lives of eligible inductees along with their friends and families and considerations for social science inquiry processes. The lottery was an attempt by the Selective Service System to move away from selection procedures that had previously forced a disproportionate number of people to enlist as correlated with attributes of "social class, race, risk tolerance, and so forth" (Johnson et al. 2019). At the same time, this process and display of *random chance*, as afforded through a lottery and live television, with its intention to perform transparency and equity regarding Selective Service, resulted in a higher incidence of voting by mothers whose sons were selected for the draft, and other systemic impacts, unfolding over several years (Johnson et al. 2019). The intentions for creating a spectacle with particular affective goals are qualified, in terms of benefits or abuses to an audience, according to how and when the impacts are analyzed and understood.

Spectacles can serve as an ideal sailing ship or freight train for ghosts to make passage across time—traveling as reverberations, and touching down at various ports of call, a whistle-stop tour for delivering stump speeches that change according to context. In some ways, spectacles align with the definition of *transmedia*—stories with multiple characters and points-of-entry and view; decentralized authorship; nonlinear plot progressions; ongoing contributions through open, generative spaces; a variety of formats and platforms for exchange; and meanings that emerge through wildly different ways of *reading* the images and narratives. The Bible is an example of transmedia and is a narrative filled with spectacles.

Spectacles operate in ways, like most narratives, that are hard to measure. The hyper-legibility and timely emergence of spectacles can be misleading in regard to causal logics within cultural conversations. Spectacles can provoke clarifying realizations toward positive outcomes and also power both benevolent and malevolent deceptions. Magicians use sleight of hand as spectacles to misdirect attention—we see *something else* while watching a magic act, or so we believe. Spectacles can take the form of a Trojan horse or a Russian doll—narratives wrapped in layers of images that obscure the affective qualities residing within their core. Alternatively, spectacles might be narratives without a determined center of meaning and serve only to provoke inquiry like a Buddhist koan.

This chapter serves as an invitation, as offered through the question: How might participatory design processes use image-oriented narratives for designing spectacles to reflect and prefigure gestures for manifesting futures with greater equity, social justice, and sustainability?

Image-oriented narratives and revolutionary ways of being

In the initial pages of Chapter 1 of this book, an anecdote by ethicist Dr. Bill Grace is shared as a provocation to imagine a world where healthy, safe, and desirable ways of existence could be accommodated anywhere and for anyone. The story features space aliens who land on Earth with plans to vaporize the planet for failure to evolve harmoniously and giving one last chance, one year, to make good by transforming society in ways so that we Earthlings are OK with the idea of transporting any child to any place on the globe. It's hyperbolic and perhaps impossible to fathom. The point is not to propose a design challenge but rather to invite the question: *Is there a crisis of imagination?*

Calamities, terrorism, outlandish marketing stunts, state violence enacted by police or armies, and celebrity pomp are some bold examples of the kinds of spectacles that seem to corner the market on attention-grabbing. The media barrage of disaster, fascist, glam, and jackass spectacles can obscure the notion that spectacles might have other profiles in terms of ethical intentions and desired outcomes. The formal characteristics of a spectacle, like the formal characteristics of narrative and design, do not necessarily qualify its affective position as ethical, "What is at issue is what or whose ethics are being expressed" (Duncombe [2007] 2019, p. 125). Stephen Duncombe, in his book *Dream or Nightmare: Reimagining Politics in an Age of Fantasy*, begins a discussion around the central features of *ethical spectacles* by first pointing out the alignment of characteristics of all spectacles, including fascism and commercialism, describing these as "looking beyond reason, rationality, and self-evident truth and making use of story, myth, fantasy, and imagination to further their respective agendas" (Duncombe [2007] 2019, p. 124). Spectacle, as a device, is effective for producing both dreams and nightmares—an ideal outcome for some that is a horror show for others, an 'image of crisis' or an 'image of change,' and so on. In the film *Rosemary's Baby*, a stylized montage of fragmented scenes invades Rosemary's sleep to represent an event of intercourse with the devil. She screams, "this is no dream! This is really happening" (Polansky 1968)! Rosemary's Satan-worshiping neighbors view the spectacle as a cause to celebrate, and her husband's career got a boost from the deal he's made on her behalf.

Given its role as a proxy for real life, cinema can challenge the notions of what might be believable, desirable, and ethical, and for whom. Cinematic tropes are the language through which moving-image narratives perform— lexicons that invite viewers to pay attention in particular ways. Like a magician's sleight of hand, cinema can misdirect attention and open new spaces for illusions to appear. Aldus Huxley in *Brave New World* presents a form of cinema that transmits physical sensations directly to the nervous system, an experience referred to as 'the feelies' (Huxley [1932] 1998). In the totalitarian, dystopian future of the novel, there is "no leisure from pleasure, not a moment to sit down and think" (Huxley 1932, cited in Frost 2006, p. 448). Movies, today, are in large part subjected to the 'capitalist-realism-of-things' that "occupies the horizons of the thinkable" and offer little in terms of insights for decision-making (Fisher 2009, cited in Bruce 2021). Escapist blockbusters, too often laden with CGI-superheroes, erase any time or space to think, glean insights, contemplate conjunctive meanings, and otherwise be moved in regard to one's perspective on life that might be afforded through cinematic tropes.

In the dramatic satire film *Network*, a frightening precursor to Fisher's *Capitalist Realism*, the actor Peter Finch plays Howard Beale, an aging TV news anchor turned mad prophet. Beale's soliloquies are coopted by the network for market-share ratings despite their rage against the corporate machine. In one iconic scene, Beale, dripping wet, steps in front of the cameras, having walked despondently through New York City rain, and delivers an impassioned speech, broadcasted live, excoriating the dystopic state of the world, and climaxing with his invitation to reflect as a way to enact a collective spectacle:

> I don't want you to protest. I don't want you to riot. I don't want you to write to your congressman, because I wouldn't know what to tell you to write. I don't know what to do about the depression and the inflation and the Russians and the crime in the street. All I know is that first, you've got to get mad. You've gotta say, "I'm a human being, goddammit! My life has value!"
>
> (Lumet, Chayefsky 1976)

Beale breaks the fourth wall during the speech. He moves out from behind the anchor's desk, forcing the cameras to follow his movements and revealing the artifice of the studio. He models the instructions that he delivers to the TV audience, to "get up right now and go to the window," freeing himself and the audience from the illusion of containment afforded through the polished surfaces of media, and to yell, "I'm mad as hell, and I'm not going to take this anymore" (Lumet, Chayefsky 1976)! Several cities where affiliate news stations are broadcasting Beale's rant report that people are screaming from their windows—the reverberations of the collective spectacle. Once Beale becomes more problematic and less profitable than corporate shareholders wish to endure, he is assassinated; Beale's violent death is merely another spectacle taking place through 'live' television, shuffled without differentiation among others taking place voluminously and simultaneously on alternative channels—a landscape of disposable narratives. The dangers of normalizing neoliberalism's perniciousness are clear and depressing.

If designers are to consider cinematic tropes as devices for engineering spectacles toward transformation, how might narratives be enduring and generative?

Arturo Escobar begins the third and final section of his book, *Designs for the Pluriverse: Radical Interdependence, Autonomy, and the Making of Worlds*, with a powerful discussion around stories and the discourse of transition. Escobar proposes transdisciplinary praxis as central to the many efforts of transition imaginaries taking place within and beyond the academy, citing Thomas Berry:

> "We are in between stories. The old story, the account of how the world came to be and how we fit into it, is no longer effective, yet we have not learned the new story" (Berry 1988, 123, cited in Escobar 2018, p. 139). The search for a new story (or rather new stories) is on: he puts it most pointedly and comprehensively: "We must describe the challenge before us with the following sentence: The historical mission of our time is to reinvent the human – at the species level, with critical reflection, with the community of life systems, in a time-development context, by means of story and shared dream experience."
>
> (Berry 1999, p. 159, cited in Escobar 2018, p. 139)

Duncombe echoes this notion and proposes that "a *progressive* ethical spectacle will be one that is directly democratic, breaks down hierarchies, fosters community, allows for diversity, and engages with reality while asking what new realities might be possible" (Duncombe [2007] 2019, p. 126).

Is there a crisis of imagination? If there is, it is certainly not for lack of output regarding images and narratives. The volume of messages and stories in the forms of books, blogs, movies, TV shows, social media posts, newsletters, and text messages is dizzying. Audre Lorde reminds us that "using the master's tools will never dismantle the master's house" (Lorde [1984] 2007, p. 110). My proposal is optimistic in its belief that spectacles do not belong to any master, and even if they did, they might be hacked, modified, and made queer in order to dismantle parts of the master's house—beginning with the boiler room of values. How might we dismantle by way of casting a luminous glow of loving care that dilutes the hierarchy of neoliberal values?

> Each technology not only differently mediates our figurations of bodily existence but also constitutes them. That is, each offers our lived bodies radically different ways of "being-in-the-world." Each implicates us in different structures of material investment, and—because each has a particular affinity with different cultural functions, forms, and contents—each stimulates us through differing modes of presentation and representation to different aesthetic responses and ethical responsibilities.
>
> (Sobchack 2004, p. 136)

Is there a crisis of imagination?

> Someone once said that it is easier to imagine the end of the world than
> to imagine the end of capitalism. We can now revise that and witness
> the attempt to imagine capitalism by way of imagining the end of the
> world.
>
> (Jameson 2003)

Is it easier to imagine the end of the world than it is to imagine a world that
includes a glimpse of extinction on the horizon, a world that might find
ways of being outside the ubiquitous belief that expansion is infinite and
growth is never ending? If there is a crisis of imagination, would we know
it or be willing to say so? Have we been traumatized by persistently rein-
forced conditions of precariousness in ways that have caused us to assimi-
late into a culture that punishes imagination (Schulman 2012)?

Spectacles with negative externalities, especially those occurring in
litigious societies, are often the objects for rallying the hunt for culpability—someone and/or something must be responsible for harm, and those
'proven' to be responsible will pay. Accountability is useful, however,
the rabid instrumentalization of spectacles as a mode for prospecting to
profit can paralyze the imaginative gestures of society for seeking ways
forward. In the film *The Sweet Hereafter*, the main spectacle—the image
of crisis—is a scene in which a school bus full of children careens off the
side of a hilly snow-packed road and gracefully slides, in a static extra-
wide shot, out onto a frozen lake where it comes to rest for a moment,
and then drops below the splintering icy surface, disappearing into the
cold water (Egoyan 1997). The film, based on a novel that was based
on a real event, follows a lawyer's attempt to put together a case for a
remunerative suit, questioning the notion of 'accident' for defining the
event. We must be careful! While no amount of care ensures movements
without flaws. Jordan Baker attempts to excuse her bad driving to Nick
Carraway in *The Great Gatsby*, while she provokes questions concerning the reciprocity and care of relationships:

> It was on that same house party that we had a curious conversation
> about driving a car. It started because she passed so close to some
> workmen that our fender flicked a button on one man's coat.
>
> "You're a rotten driver," I protested. 'Either you ought to be more
> careful or you oughtn't to drive at all.'
>
> "I am careful."
>
> "No, you're not."
>
> "Well, other people are," she said lightly.

'What's that got to do with it?'

"They'll keep out of my way," she insisted. "It takes two to make an accident."

"Suppose you met somebody just as careless as yourself."

"I hope I never will," she answered. "I hate careless people. That's why I like you."

(Fitzgerald, F.S. [1925] 2004, p. 58)

What might a world organized with care as the priority look like?

Unreliable narrators can serve as useful guides for moving through mysterious and unknown worlds while seeking paths of transformation. In several of the spectacular communiques from the Zapatistas as issued by Subcomandante Marcos, Durito—a spectacle-wearing, pipe-smoking, talking beetle—features as the protagonist. Durito is first encountered in a short story by Marcos that he wrote as a response to a letter from a ten-year-old girl. Marcos recounts his initial meeting with Durito:

"And you, what is your name?" I asked him.

"Nebuchadnezzar," he said, and continued, "but my friends call me Durito. You can call me Durito, Captain."

I thanked him for the courtesy and asked him what it was that he was studying.

"I'm studying neoliberalism and its strategy of domination for Latin America," he told me.

"And what good is that to a beetle?" I asked him.

And he replied, very annoyed: "What *good* is it? I have to know how long your struggle is going to last, and whether you are going to win. Besides, a beetle should care enough to study the situation of the world in which it lives, don't you think, captain?"

"I don't know," I said. "But, why do you want to know how long our struggle will last and whether or not we are going to win?"

"Well, you haven't understood a thing," he told me, putting on his glasses and lighting his pipe. After letting out a puff of smoke, "To know how long we beetles are going to have to take care that you do not smash us with your big boots."

(Subcomandante Insurgente Marcos 2005, pp. 42–43)

Egyptians celebrated the scarab as a supreme symbol of transformation, protection, and immortality, as they observed the dung beetle as a creature that emerged from the earth, a symbol of birth, life, and resurrection of the dead (Ward 1994). The insurgency of the Zapatistas is rooted in the land—land reform, Indigenous agrarian identity, and dignity through autonomy (Conant 2010). Termites, like beetles, burrow at the foundations and chip away at boundaries to create opportunistic paths. Perhaps a more palatable illustration of resistance and rebirth is through the narrations of insects—'fables of the reconstruction,' to borrow a term from the title of an R.E.M record album (R.E.M. 1985).

Cinema, like spectacle, comes in radically different sizes. The power of 'small cinema' as evidenced in the 21st century is discussed by Dennis Lim in the article "The Termite's Return," referencing Manny Farber's article from the early 1960s, "White Elephant Art vs. Termite Art" (Lim 2020). Lim writes,

> Today, however, it seems easier than ever to identify both the white elephants for which art is (as he [Farber] put it) "an expensive hunk of well-regulated area"—the prestige movie by the brand-name auteur, the festival film with its pre-digested meanings—and the countervailing termite tendencies of work that "goes always forward eating its own boundaries" and "feels its way through walls of particularization."
>
> (Farber 1962, cited in Lim 2020)

Television has long been experimenting with termite strategies inside of its elephants, for example, the pioneering work of producer Miguel Sabido. Sabido integrated social agendas within long narrative arcs of Mexican telenovelas during the 1970s. The para-social relationships with fictional characters were the vehicles of trust that the viewers of telenovelas relied upon while facing difficult decisions and struggling to make changes in their own lives (Rosin 2006). Sit-coms created by Norman Lear in the United States followed a similar path, except that Lear's satirical provocations played as bombastic hijinks with social-change messages intricately woven through jokes serving as Trojan horses for morality lessons. Lear's award-winning TV show *All in the Family*, premiering in 1971, featured the bigoted character Archie Bunker as a catalyst for the positive transformations of those characters around him (Freeman 2017).

"Revolutionary thinking means focusing on the frame rather than on the goodies within it, but reality means doing this to the extent that you can without being victimized by the folks who don't want to be accountable" (Schulman 2012, p. 164). So, what might a termite-progressing ethical spectacle look like today?

Co-creating spectacles and prefigurative gestures

Engaging in ritual, modeling behavior, learning in cooperative settings, embodying revolution, and other modes of celebrating forward momentum are acts of both strategic consciousness and somewhat blind leaps of faith that can prefigure future society. Here are a few projects that point toward directions for a more just, equitable, and sustainable world through proposals of participatory design-based spectacles.

Queering the economy with cakes

Hannah Rose Fox investigated an experimental model for a queer economy through baking and sharing 20 cakes over a period of six months. Fox meticulously calculated labor and material costs in efforts to contrast the limits of traditional measurements of value with the expanded value created through social and gift exchanges. The experiment was conducted while Fox was a student in the Transdisciplinary Design program at Parsons School of Design and informed her thesis work. She describes the project as, "*Cakeonomies* points to how we might shift away from our emphasis on limited forms of measurement, value as created by material and labor alone, binary understandings of exchange practices, and finite resources as endpoints in networks" (Fox 2021). The project is also an experiment for queering time within capitalist economic practices through the disruption of expectations that are concretized by way of heteronormative ideas in terms of life's milestones. Typical occasions where cakes serve as emblems of reward for time-based systems—weddings, birthdays, retirement parties, and other celebrations that valorize 'accomplishments' within capitalist regimes of counting—are ignored and up-ended through random acts of gifting cakes. Fox sometimes gifted cakes without a prior relationship with recipients, leaving introductions and instructions with a cake on doorstep. The experiment also asked participants to contribute reflections regarding these moments of cake- and exchange-value.

Trashy raves, Litterally

Leveraging the expressive gestures of dance performance as a mode of wilding, and akin to traditions of carnival, *Litterally* is a street action by Alexa Gantous and part of her larger project called *Trash Talk*. Gantous utilizes the spectacle of collective performance to address and reframe relationships with waste. Literally dancing in the streets while picking up trash, these events feature Gantous leading troupes of friends and colleagues through New York City neighborhoods in gleeful displays of bagging garbage, as shown in Figure 4.1. Their weekly appearance and proximity to pedestrians and onlookers from stoops, balconies, and windows sparks curiosity. Social media sharing of these spectacular events cultivates their comic and cosmic mythologies and promotes the roving refuse warriors turned flash-mob

Figure 4.1 Litterally event, designed and led by Alexa Gantous, (right), 2019.

circuit party to mobilize a growing number of participants. Gantous infuses the project's narrative with her infectious cadence of optimism. Her exuberance and charming tone serve as a delightful hack of traditional shaming tactics—*why wouldn't we pick up this mess we've made?* Gantous extends the conversation to address the gravity of waste through salon-style gatherings as well as a podcast series, *Trash Talk*, she produces and hosts. Alexa Gantous developed *Litterally* and *Trash Talk* while a student in the Strategic Design and Management BBA program at Parsons School of Design.

Go Light, $150 for a phone that does nothing

The original Light Phone, co-founded by Joe Hollier and Kaiwei Tang, is a simple phone with very limited functionality—a dumb phone for making and receiving phone calls only. I first encountered the co-founders and their idea during a pitch session as part of the 30 Weeks Google-sponsored incubator program in 2015. Sitting in the audience of about 200 people, I was simultaneously overcome with laughter and intrigue by Joe Hollier's performative introduction. He walked onto the stage, holding a credit-card-sized piece of cardboard in the air and said: "This is a phone. It makes phone calls." The atmosphere in the room shifted. After having witnessed a series of other pitches about projects focused on virtual visits and clicks,

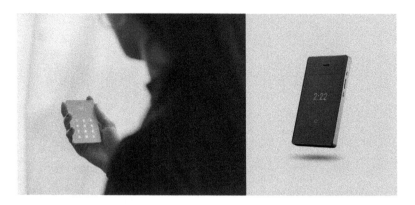

Figure 4.2 The Light Phone, (left), and Light Phone II, (right), designed by Joe Hollier and Kaiwei Tang, 2017.

the audience was now paying attention differently, delightedly. In 2017, following a successful crowd-funding event, many months of engineering, and some angel investments, the Light Phone, as shown in Figure 4.2, became available to consumers as a way to be less distracted and more present in life by leaving your smartphone behind for a few hours. (Full disclosure, I have served as a strategic advisor to this company.) One of the primary value propositions is the brand's cinematic style for leading the cultural conversation concerning the strained capacity to *pay attention to our attention*. The Light Phone brand centers the design invitation to 'go light'—to be free from virtual hyper-connectivity through breaking the addiction of 'checking' that is brought about by the mini-computer turned FOMO slot-machine now in nearly everyone's pocket. The tagline 'designed to be used as little as possible' serves to anchor to the brand's promise while antithetical to perhaps most business models for communication tech (Hollier, Tang 2021).

An early advertising campaign utilized street flyers drawn by Hollier to reflect pain points with humor and mysterious provocation. One flyer featured the text, "Dear time, please slow down. Thanks, Joe," along with a unique URL ineedmore.me, linking to a landing webpage citing a brief manifesto about 'going light' that included the URL to the Light Phone product webpage. Another flyer featured the image of a banana phone and the words 'GO LIGHT' hovering over 'WARNING WARNING,' above an image of an arm reaching out from a smartphone, as shown in Figure 4.3. The campaign comprised several different images, slogans, and provocative unique URLS, like avoidthehole.com, referring to the 'scroll hole' of

Figure 4.3 The Light Phone flyer campaigns, designed by Joe Hollier, 2017.

mindless surfing on social sharing phone apps and utilized a strategy of
slight strangeness—the *familiar* mixed with a few odd twists to disrupt
expectations. The Light Phone flyers did not show or promote the Light
phone directly. The messages were unclear in their transactional purpose
while offering relatable narratives. Promo videos made by Hollier show
'going light' lifestyle vignettes from pristine nature settings to quiet
moments at home or in and around cities. The aesthetics exude living well
by design through intentionally *not adding more* stuff and distractions. It is
the design which takes away that which is not needed and creates space for
new encounters and new ways for learning. The Light Phone II, shown in
Figure 4.2, is a winner of the Good Design® 2021 Award. It costs around
twice as much as the first Light Phone, offers more features, and is perhaps
less light yet more tenable for staying in the mix while still avoiding the
scroll hole. The Light Phone blog features stories about the production of
the device, Light's manifesto, a sustainability report, a billboard message to
Apple CEO Tim Cook, and other points of information beyond just trying
to sell you something (Hollier, Tang 2021).

Library workers and radical hospitality

Public libraries are one of the few places in our society that offer opportunities to engage with people, share services, and exchange resources
without structural partitions or economic demands. I served as the
lead ethnographer for the Parsons DESIS Lab collaboration with the

Brooklyn Public Library (BPL), an investigation focused on designing systems to support the services provided to communities, especially those impacted by incarceration. DESIS stands for Design for Social Innovation and Sustainability and is a network of more than 50 chapters across the world (DESIS Network 2021). The findings from our field-work revealed the myriad of ways that library workers at BPL serve as agents of radical hospitality (Penin et al. 2019). Hospitality extends protection, enables survival, fosters connectedness, and conveys respect. It converts strangers into familiars and repositions outsiders as insiders. As such, it is deeply entwined with modes of caring. The Bedford Branch of BPL served as the main site of our participatory research and features an open, accessible, and socially accommodating reference desk. Entering the Bedford branch, patrons are confronted with convivial service within a casual atmosphere of care. On one day while our research team was present, a patron collapsed near the entrance. The staff, familiar with the patron and his particular physical challenges, reacted with calm and graceful gestures like a well-choreographed performance. The scenario was a spectacle of dignity and solidarity. The library workers at the Bedford branch of BPL were key interlocutors for our research, and one in particular, Elaine Smalls, became a co-ethnographer, as shown in Figure 4.4. Elaine's affinity for using the camera, coupled with her

Figure 4.4 Elaine Smalls, Brooklyn Public Library staff and co-ethnographer, 2020.

intuitive sense for deep listening to recognize the nuanced complexity of people's needs, made Elaine an invaluable part of our research team. Elaine had worked at BPL for 25 years, knew most of the patrons personally, and shared her wisdom in more ways than simply helping people locate books. Elaine's journey of being guided by people who shared information with her during pivotal moments of her life informs the expanded notions of knowledge sharing she brings to her role at BPL. Elaine and other library workers at BPL extend services for immigrants, elders, the unhoused, and those transitioning out of correctional systems—they intervene where other services fail or are absent. In doing so—because the library is an institution without stigma—parameters of alliance are redrawn.

New worlds of presence and participation

Two weeks before his death on October 24, 2020, artist Matt Freedman participated in a final session with the *End of Life* project—the artistic research that I have been leading with Pawel Wojtasik. We had worked with Matt since 2014, during which time his life as an artist, university professor, husband, amateur volleyball player, improv actor, and all-around fun person to be with seemed largely unaffected by terminal cancer he suffered from. However, during the summer and autumn of 2020, Matt's health was in rapid decline, yet he remained eager to continue living and working as an artist. On the last day of our collaboration together, he rendered a series of three-dimensional drawings in virtual reality (VR) environment using Oculus Quest equipment, as shown in Figure 4.5. This was only the second time he had ever used these technologies. Our process utilized the Spatial .io application—a virtual environment—both as a space for developing a new artwork and for hosting a public art performance by Matt. Confined to a chair and attached to a feeding tube and oxygen supply, Matt's mobility and sociality were severely limited. Despite the challenges he encountered during this period of dying, VR technologies presented a unique opportunity for Matt to access new and renewed ways for practicing as an artist, and for these activities to provide social vitality and embodied learning through real-time virtual engagements. In VR, Matt was able to perform his experiences with illness and mortality without being contained within the limits of disease and dying. His able-bodied avatar could reflexively engage with his mortality in ways that confronted dying head on and thus served to model a unique process for audiences to in turn explore their own reflections concerning mortality. As the avatar 'endlessmatt,' as shown in Figure 4.6, Matt made three-dimensional drawings in Spatial.io where others could be present and interact with him. These kinds of reciprocal exchanges formed

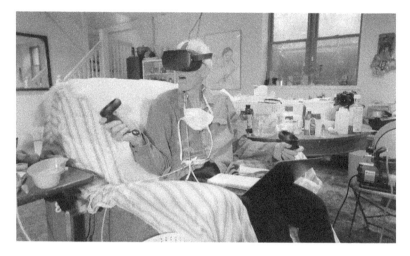

Figure 4.5 Matt Freedman at home using VR to make drawings, October 10, 2020.

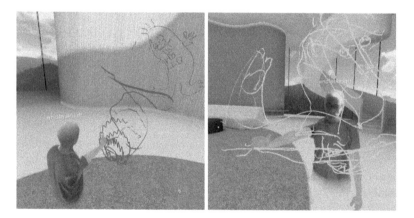

Figure 4.6 Matt Freedman as avatar "endlessmatt" making drawings in a VR environment.

the basis for pedagogy that celebrate living while dying and thus work to collapse the distances created around end-of-life experiences. The use of VR for designing conditions where embodied learning can take place holds great promise for alleviating suffering for the dying and for the people close to and supporting their situations.

Worlding in the expanded field

While teaching the course Cinematic Tropes as Design Process at The New School, I invite students to use image-oriented narrative devices without the care afforded to make a good film for people to watch and enjoy. I promote practices for taking liberties while employing cinematic tropes as part of design processes that privileges participatory means rather than end products. Rarely are any of the students in this course studying to become filmmakers. The commonality shared among the students is reflected through The New School's mission of equity, inclusion, and social justice. Our learning together is making together and without limits on our imagination. Within a learning community, how might we build capacities for endeavoring imaginative gestures of world-making together? Worlding is sympoieses.

> Sympoiesis is a simple word; it means "making-with." Nothing makes itself; nothing is really autopoietic or self-organizing. In the words of the Inupiat computer "world game," earthlings are *never alone*. That is the radical implication of sympoiesis. *Sympoiesis* is a word proper to complex, dynamic, responsive, situated, historical systems. It is a word for worlding-with, in company. Sympoiesis enfolds autopoiesis and generatively unfurls and extends it.
>
> (Haraway 2016, p. 58)

Margaret Wheatley paraphrasing Rudolf Bahro, a German activist and iconoclast, describes worlding when the world needs it most as a time, "When the forms of an old culture are dying, the new culture is created by a few people who are not afraid to be insecure" (Wheatley 2009). Ram Dass says, start with yourself and see if 'the world' or one's world changes (Ram Dass [1971] 1978). I remain curious and optimistic in pondering the ways design tries too hard or not hard enough. Perhaps design works hard in the wrong directions—spends too much time reverse-engineering problems, or does so through a solution-based lens; perhaps design employs aesthetics in ways unconscious of affect; strives for didacticism while ignoring complexity; thinks only to add and never to take away; demands clarity too often at the expense of poetry; and becomes unsure of itself unless there are boxes that can be checked, processes that can be replicated, and impacts that can be measured. My colleague Elliott Montgomery at The New School is fond of asking design students how design might emerge through and be imbued with both audacity and humility. Phil Ronniger, a life coach and educator (who was my career counselor while I was a graduate student), teaches about the notion of *I don't know*. How might we build collectives where we can really get into what it means not to know, together? Unlearning and relearning. When I first met Phil, I *really did not know* in ways that made me pretty angry. He instructed me to write 25 stories that reflected events from my life highlighting positive moments of achievement, learning, relationships, community, and career, as defined by me. I wrote 27 stories in about four weeks. Phil helped me synthesize the findings, not so much as creating a map but rather polishing a mirror. It was the most powerful reflection exercise I have ever endeavored—a way to practice the ubiquitous Didion quote, "We tell ourselves stories in order to live" (Didion 1979, p. 11). Most importantly, it helped me *get good* with really *not knowing* a lot of the time. From here, more space opens up to imagine together. Let's imagine a community where care, or perhaps water, is valued most—all decisions are based on relationships with this priority to render conditions for healthy, safe, enjoyable ways of life for all in the community. Let's imagine more collective pirate acts—hacking, queering, modifying, and less ego-driven fantasies of individual heroism. Let's imagine less competitive accumulation and more collectively decided upon distribution of the surplus. Let's imagine the potential value of entropy, for instance, any kind of 'marriage' of sorts might be embraced as a success even if it doesn't end in death. Let's imagine capacities for being with groundlessness, welcoming the swift currents, looking around to see who's with us, and celebrating. Let's imagine space where poets and engineers gather and break bread. Let's work more with the cracks, the between-ness, the *Ma*, and less with the *me*. In the ways that Manhattanites are not far from Nauru, US citizens are not far from Afghanistan, or any of us far from the places we might be dropped by space aliens into another context on the globe, as a way to bolster our accountability for participating in efforts for a more equitable and just future.

Making decisions is at the core of activities for producing art and design. Stated in this way, creative endeavors sound much less mysterious and romantic, and certainly less glamorous. How might decision-making be informed for producing the kinds of images and narratives that imagine a more just and equitable future? Photography and movie making are also acts of love. Let's indulge the notion of participatory design as approached through thoughtful and collective encounters with images and narrative: being with people to watch a movie or a play, experiencing art, and thinking about it; making things together, reflecting, and becoming together. Spectacles can emerge.

References

Berry, T. (1988) *The Dream of the Earth*, San Francisco, CA: Sierra Club Books.
Bruce, J.A. (2021) Mortality. In Eduardo Staszowski and Virginia Tassinari, eds. *Designing in Dark Times: An Arendtian Lexicon*, London: Bloomsbury, pp. 195–198.

Conant, J. (2010) *A Poetics of Resistance: The Revolutionary Public Relations of the Zapatista Insurgency*, Oakland, CA: AK Press.

DESIS Network (2021) *DESIS Network*, Retrieved from https://www.desisnetwork.org/.

Didion, J. (1979) *The White Album*, New York: Simon and Schuster.

Duncombe, S. (2019 [2007]) *Dream or Nightmare: Reimagining Politics in an Age of Fantasy*, New York, NY: OR Books.

Egoyan, A. (Director) (1997) *The Sweet Hereafter*, Canada: Alliance Communications.

Escobar, A. (2018) *Designs for the Pluriverse: Radical Interdependence, Autonomy, and the Making of Worlds*, Durham: Duke University Press.

Farber, M. (1962/3) White Elephant Art vs. Termite Art. In Jonas Mekas, ed. *Film Culture* 27, Winter.

Fisher, M. (2009) *Capitalist Realism*, London: Zero Books.

Fitzgerald, F.S. (2004 [1925]) *The Great Gatsby*, New York, NY: Scribner.

Freeman, M. (2017) Norman Lear on How "All in the Family" Gave Birth to Political Sitcoms. *The Hollywood Reporter*, December 26. Retrieved from https://www.hollywoodreporter.com/tv/tv-news/norman-lear-how-all-family-gave-birth-political-sitcoms-1069768/.

Frost, L. (2006) Huxley's Feelies: The Cinema of Sensation in "Brave New World". *Twentieth Century Literature* 52(4), pp. 443–473.

Fox, H. (2021) *Cakeonomie*, unpublished thesis project, MFA Transdisciplinary Design program, Parsons School of Design.

Haraway, D. (2016) *Staying with the Trouble: Making Kin in the Chthulucene*, Durham: Duke University Press.

Hollier, J., Tang, K. (2021) *Light Phone*. Retrieved from www.thelightphone.com.

Huxley, A. (1998 [1932]) *Brave New World*, New York, NY: Harper.

Jameson, F. (2003) Future City. *New Left Review* 21, May–June. Retrieved from https://newleftreview.org/issues/ii21/articles/fredric-jameson-future-city.

Johnson, T., Conley, D., Dawes, C.T. (2019) The Accidental Experiment That Changed Men's Lives. *The Atlantic*, December 2. Retrieved from https://www.theatlantic.com/science/archive/2019/12/vietnam-draft-lotteries-were-scientific-experiment/602842/.

Lim, D. (2020) The Termite's Return: Reflecting on an Unwieldy Decade in Film, from the Ground Up. *Film Comment*, January. Retrieved from https://www.filmcomment.com/article/the-termites-return-dennis-lim-best-of-the-decade/.

Lorde, A. (2007 [1984]) *Sister Outsider: Essays and Speeches*, Berkeley, CA: Crossing Press.

Lumet, S., Chayefsky, P. (Director), (Writer) (1976) *Network*, US: United Artists.

Penin, L., Staszowski, E., Bruce, J.A., Adams, B., Amatullo, M. (2019) Public Libraries as Engines of Democracy: A Research and Pedagogical Case Study on Design for Re-Entry. In T. Mattelmäki, R. Maze, S. Miettinen, N. Chun, eds. *Who Cares? Proceedings of the 8th Biannual Nordic Design Research Society*, Espoo: Aalto University School. Available online: https://archive.nordes.org/index.php/n13/issue/view/13

Polansky, R. (Director) (1968) *Rosemary's Baby*, Los Angeles, US: Paramount Pictures.

Ram Dass (1978 [1971]) *Be Here Now*, San Cristobal, New Mexico: Hanuman Foundation.

R.E.M. (Recording artists) (1985) *Fables of the Reconstruction*, US: IRS Records.

Rosin, H. (2006) Life Lessons: How Soap Operas Can Change the World. *The New Yorker*, June 5.

Schulman, S. (2012) *The Gentrification of the Mind: Witness to a Lost Imagination.* Berkeley, CA: University of California Press.

Sobchack, V. (2004) *Carnal Thoughts: Embodiment and Moving Image Culture*, Berkeley, CA: University of California Press.

spectacle (2010) *Oxford Dictionary of English*, 2nd ed., Oxford, Engalnd: Oxford University Press.

Subcomandante Insurgente Marcos (2005) *Conversations with Durito: Stories of Zapatistas and Neoliberalism*, Brooklyn, NY: Autonomedia.

Ward, W.A. (1994) Beetles in Stone: The Egyptian Scarab. *The Biblical Archaeologist* 57(4), pp. 186–202.

Wheatley, Margaret (2009) The Place Beyond Fear and Hope. *Shambhala Sun*, March, p. 81.

Index

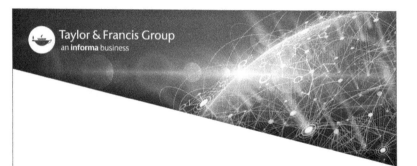